Data Structures and Algorithms in C++

Pocket Primer

LICENSE, DISCLAIMER OF LIABILITY, AND LIMITED WARRANTY

Data Structures and Algorithms in C++

Pocket Primer

Lee Wittenberg

MERCURY LEARNING AND INFORMATION
Dulles, Virginia
Boston, Massachusetts
New Delhi

Publisher: David Pallai
MERCURY LEARNING AND INFORMATION
22841 Quicksilver Drive
Dulles, VA 20166
info@merclearning.com
www.merclearning.com
(800) 232-0223

Lee Wittenberg. *Data Structures and Algorithms in C++*: Pocket Primer.
ISBN: 978-1-68392-084-7

The publisher recognizes and respects all marks used by companies, manufacturers, and developers as a means to distinguish their products. All brand names and product names mentioned in this book are trademarks or service marks of their respective companies. Any omission or misuse (of any kind) of service marks or trademarks, etc. is not an attempt to infringe on the property of others.

Library of Congress Control Number: 2017934713

171819321   Printed in the United States of America
This book is printed on acid-free paper.

Our titles are available for adoption, license, or bulk purchase by institutions, corporations, etc.

For additional information, please contact the Customer Service Dept. at (800) 232-0223 (toll free). Digital versions of our titles are available at: www.authorcloudware.com and other e-vendors. Companion files for this title may be requested at info@merclearning.com.

CONTENTS

PREFACE

This book is a data structures textbook stripped down to the essentials. It includes only those topics that are absolutely necessary in an introductory data structures course, and omits everything else. The topics are presented in such a way that you might retain the vital points, and eventually, understand the complete contents. It should be appropriate both for students just getting started (having only a basic knowledge of programming) and professionals wanting a brief "refresher course."

PLAN OF ATTACK

The book is focused on fundamental data structures, the algorithms associated with them, and their implementation in C++, with particular emphasis on the relationship of these data structures to those in the C++ Standard Template Library (STL). To that end, most chapters follow the same pattern:

1. A description of the data structure itself.

2. A description of the relevant STL interface, but only those functions that are absolutely necessary for an understanding of the structure.

3. One or more examples of how the data structure might be used in practice. These examples are in the form of algorithms, rather than C++ code.

4. A complete implementation of the data structure, based on the described STL interface. To avoid confusion with the types defined in the STL, I name my versions with an initial capital letter (e.g., Vector rather than vector).

The implementations are not necessarily the best, nor do they adhere to "standard" STL implementation techniques. The focus here is on the data structure itself, not on the STL. The code also follows the "minimalist" approach: just enough to help you understand what's "under the hood." New C++ concepts are introduced only when absolutely necessary.

The STL makes great use of all the facilities of the C++ programming language, most of which are not necessary for an understanding of the underlying data structures. For example, the member function `size` returns an unsigned value of type `size_type`, which is usually the same as another unsigned type called `size_t` (don't ask). In this book, I use `int` for all integral types, whether signed or not. Unless a data structure contains a huge number of elements, the difference between signed and unsigned integer types isn't relevant, and can only complicate explanations. In keeping with the minimalist approach, no advanced features of the language are used when a more basic one will do.

EXERCISES

Most computer science texts have a multitude of questions and exercises at the end of each chapter. You can learn more by focusing on one relatively complex problem dealing with a chapter's concepts than by working on a lot of smaller, simpler problems. To that end, each chapter ends with a single exercise. Some of these exercises require implementing some data structure, but most involve *using* the data structure or concept described in the chapter. Working these problems will help you understand what you need to understand and remember what you need to remember.

REFERENCES

In lieu of a traditional bibliography, I have supplied Appendix A (A Programmer's Library), a reasonably short list of the books every computer scientist should own (and, at least, glance through from time to time). These titles appear (or should appear) in the bibliographies of other data structures texts. Whenever it is important where a particular concept originated, I point that out. For everything else, the best source is almost certainly Donald Knuth's *Art of Computer Programming* (see Appendix A), and if it isn't, it probably will be once the final volume is published.

SAMPLE CODE

While the sample code in this book adheres (mostly) to the standard commonly known as C++03, there are a few features of the newer C++11 standard that are important enough to use. As of this writing, not all C++ compilers have fully implemented the C++11 standard, so I explicitly note those features as they are introduced in the text. When appropriate, I also explain how to accomplish the same thing in C++03.

Some readers may not be familiar with the standard keywords and, or, and not, which are are used here in place of the more traditional '&&', '||', and '!' symbols.* The keywords are exactly equivalent to the corresponding symbols.

The C++ code in the text demonstrates a technique called *literate programming* to describe the code, using a collection of software tools called noweb.† This makes it possible to explain a small bit of code and show that code (called a *chunk*) immediately after, using English placeholders for those bits that are not yet ready to be committed to code.

For example, suppose that we want to do something or other when a given condition is true,

⟨*sample code chunk*⟩≡
```
if ((⟨given condition⟩)) {
    ⟨do something or other⟩
}
```

and let's say the given condition is that the value of x is less than the value of y,

⟨*given condition*⟩≡
```
x < y
```

and what we want to do in that case is to swap the values of x and y.

⟨*do something or other*⟩≡
```
swap(x, y);
```

If we then wish to assign the value f(b) to a after the if statement, we simply append the new statement to the ⟨*sample code chunk*⟩ chunk. This is indicated by the +≡ symbol in place of ≡ in the chunk definition.

⟨*sample code chunk*⟩+≡
```
a = f(b);
```

The chunks can be *tangled* to produce the source code that will be processed by a compiler. This is much like the process of "stepwise refinement" that you learned in your introductory programming classes, except that it is done automatically by a tool called notangle, instead of by hand. When tangled, ⟨*sample code chunk*⟩ produces the following:

---

*The Microsoft compiler in Visual Studio, however, does not support these keywords by default. You have to "turn off Microsoft extensions" or #include <ciso646> before the compiler will accept them. The source code on the companion disc does the latter automatically when Visual Studio is used.

†noweb was developed by Norman Ramsey. Details are on the noweb web page: http://www.cs.tufts.edu/~nr/noweb/.

```
if (x > y) {
    swap(x, y);
}
a = f(b);
```

Most books that include sample code import the code from fully-tested source files. This one, however, uses notangle to generate the source files directly from the text. Another tool, called noweave, is used to *weave* the text (and code) into the typeset version you're reading now. It also generates the cross-reference information you'll see in the code chunks that follow.

Each chunk is labeled with its page number and an indication of where on the page the chunk occurs. For example, chunk 21a is the first chunk on page 21, and chunk 28c is the third chunk on page 28. Continuation chunks (those indicated by a += symbol in the chunk definition) are labeled with the page number and location of the original chunk in the continuation chain. Appendix C contains a list of all the chunk names used in the book, showing where each chunk is both defined and used.

The code in this book has been compiled and tested with both the GNU C++ compiler, g++ (versions 5.3.1 and 6.1.1), using the command-line options "-std=c++11" (use the C++11 standard) and "-Wall," (enable all warning messages); and the Visual Studio 2015 compiler using the options "/Za" (disable Microsoft extensions) and "/EHsc" (use standard C++ exception handling; this option is set by default in the IDE, but not by the command-line compiler). No errors or warning messages should be generated when compiling with these options. The code should also compile properly without them, but there may be warning messages. The valgrind utility was used to ensure that there were no memory leaks.

All of the code appearing in this book is available on the companion disc or for downloading from the publisher.

ACKNOWLEDGMENTS

I would like to thank Randy Meyers, Greg Weinstein, and Robert Lowe, who all gave feedback on the early drafts. Thanks are also due to my CSC 241 students, who helped to "field test" the book. Evan Ezell deserves special mention for his ability to ferret out typographical errors.

I would also like to thank David Pallai, Jennifer Blaney, and the rest of the staff at Mercury Learning for their help and support in making this book possible. I must also thank William McAllister for introducing me to them.

CHAPTER 1

C++ REVIEW

D ifferent introductory programming courses cover the various C++
language topics differently. This chapter is an attempt to make
sure we are all "on the same page" before proceeding further. You
should already be comfortable with the basic C++ types int, bool, char,
and (to a lesser extent) double; the predefined class string; expressions;
functions; input/output; and the if, while, for and do flow-of-control
constructs. Everything else you need is explained briefly in this chapter.

Most (if not all) of these topics are things you've already been exposed
to (whether or not you remember). For what you've already seen, let this
chapter serve as a gentle reminder. For whatever is new to you, take some
time to refer to your other books for fuller explanations. These are not in
any depth, and are meant mainly to jog your memory.

1.1 THE AUTO KEYWORD

The first (possibly) new concept is the C++11 definition of the auto
keyword, which allows the compiler to infer the type of a variable from
the type of its initial value. This is mostly useful in declaring for loop
"counter" variables. For example, the traditional

```
for (int i = 0; i < n; i++) { ⟨do something or other⟩ }
```

can now be written as

```
for (auto i = 0; i < n; i++) { ⟨do something or other⟩ }
```

While this example does not demonstrate any real advantage, auto will be
invaluable once we start dealing with iterators (Section 1.6.2).

While there are other possible uses for `auto` in C++11, they are somewhat problematic and error-prone, so you should restrict its use to loop control variables, iterators in particular.

1.2 CLASSES

In the same way that functions allow you to use your own verbs in a C++ program, classes allow you to use your own nouns. You can write a payroll processing program, for example, in terms of employees, supervisors, checks, etc., rather than having to reduce everything down to existing types (`int`, `bool`, `char`, and so on). Use the `class` keyword to define precisely what you mean by "employee," "supervisor," "check," or whatever other noun you want to use. The goal, as with functions, is to reduce the number of conceptual steps between your ideas and the expression of those ideas in code. Each class creates an *abstract data type*, a simplification of the concept embodied by that type allowing it to be manipulated in a program.

Every class has two parts: a public *interface* and a private *implementation*. The interface consists mostly of *declarations* for the class *member functions*, and the implementation consists of *definitions* for these functions and the *data members*. By convention, the interface goes into a file with a `.h` (for "header") extension, and the implementation into a file with a `.cpp` extension.

Every such `.h` file has the same layout. For example, if we are creating an interface for `Some_Class`, we would write

⟨*some-class.h* 2⟩≡
```
#ifndef SOME_CLASS_H
#define SOME_CLASS_H

    ⟨#include's needed for Some_Class interface⟩
    ⟨interface for Some_Class⟩

#endif
```
This code is written to file `some-class.h`.

The identifier `SOME_CLASS_H` is called a *guard*, and serves to prevent the same header file from being accidentally included by a source file more than once (which the compiler doesn't like). By using this guard, even a silly mistake like

```
#include "some-type.h"
#include "some-type.h"
```

in a single file cannot cause problems. There is no standard way to name these guards. Many programmers use the class name in all capitals followed by an underscore and a capital **H**, but you may use any convention that you like, keeping in mind that you want to choose something unlikely to be used as an identifier by some other programmer who might use your class (and has to **#include** your header). Using a hyphen in the file name instead of the class name's underscore is simply a matter of personal preference (and works better with some literate programming tools). There is no standard convention; you may name your files anything you like (but it's better if the file name bears some resemblance to the class name).

Since the "wrappers" for header files are always the same, they will not be mentioned again (but they are, of course, included in the sample code on the companion disc).

The `.cpp` files also have a regular layout:

⟨*some-class.cpp* 3a⟩≡

   ⟨**#include***'s needed for* Some_Class *implementation*⟩
   #include "some-class.h"

   using namespace std;

   ⟨*implementation of* Some_Class⟩

This code is written to file some-class.cpp.

which also is the same for every such file, and will also be omitted from the text hereafter. Note that the `.cpp` file must **#include** its corresponding `.h`, and that the directive "**using namespace std**" appears only in the `.cpp` file, not in the `.h`. This avoids the clutter of a lot of **std::** prefixes in the code. However, some programmers do not care for the **using** directive, and prefer to specify the prefix explicity wherever it is needed. You should always use the **std::** prefix when necessary in `.h` files to avoid imposing your will on the others who **#include** your code.

1.2.1 Example: A Fraction **Class**

As an example, let's look at a class that allows us to manipulate exact fractions like $\frac{1}{3}$ rather than approximate floating point values like .33333.

The Interface

The interface is laid out like this:

⟨*interface for* Fraction 3b⟩≡

   class Fraction {
   public:
      ⟨Fraction *constructor declarations* 4⟩
      ⟨Fraction *member function declarations* 5a⟩
   private:
      ⟨Fraction *data members and private function declarations* 7b⟩
   };

Technically, the data members are part of the implementation, not the interface, but the compiler needs them to be part of the class declaration in the .h file.

What we'd like to be able to do with this class is to write code like:

```
Fraction a(1, 3), b(2, 5);   // a ← 1/3, b ← 2/5
Fraction c = a + b;          // c ← a + b (= 11/15)
cout << "a = " << a << "; b = " << b
     << "; c = " << c << " => " << c.reciprocal()
     << endl;
```

which should produce the following output:

```
a = 1/3; b = 2/5; c = 11/15 => 15/11
```

We need to know how we are going to use a class before we can think of designing its interface, much less implementing it. From this simple example, we can see that we'll want the standard arithmetic operators ('+', '-', '*' and '/') as well as the '<<' output operator. We should also provide unary '+' and '-', and the relational operators '==', '!=', '>', '>=', '<', and '<='.

But first, we need to think about the *constructors*, member functions that use the name of the class to create `Fraction` objects when we need them. The above example uses a constructor with two integer parameters, representing the fraction's numerator and denominator, respectively. It's (almost) always useful to have a "default" constructor (one with no parameters). It also makes sense to have a constructor that takes a single integer parameter and constructs a `Fraction` equivalent to that integer (i.e., with a denominator of 1), which can also be used to to automatically convert an integer value into an equivalent `Fraction` (so we can use expressions in our code like `a + 1`, where a is a `Fraction`). It would seem that we need three constructors.

However, C++ allows us to specify *default arguments* for parameters, values that are used when a parameter is not specified in a function call. If we define a single two-parameter constructor with 0 as the default value for the first parameter and 1 for the second, we get a default constructor that produces $\frac{0}{1}$, a single-parameter constructor that produces $\frac{n}{1}$, as well as our original two-parameter constructor that produces $\frac{n}{d}$. In C++, a constructor is declared like a function, except that it uses the name of the class as its name and it has no return type. We declare our single constructor:

⟨Fraction *constructor declarations* 4⟩≡
```
    Fraction(int n = 0, int d = 1);
```

A little thought (and some noodling around with more examples of code we'd like to be able to write) gives us the "numerator," "denominator," and "reciprocal" member functions. These are known as *accessor* functions, because they do not change the value of any of the object's data members (they only *access* them). Accessor functions are always marked as "const."

⟨Fraction *member function declarations* 5a⟩≡
```
int numerator() const;
int denominator() const;
Fraction reciprocal() const;
```

It seems useful to provide an accessor (called "value") that returns the double value approximately equal to the Fraction, as well.

⟨Fraction *member function declarations* 5a⟩+≡
```
double value() const;
```

We can also provide a *mutator* function, "invert," which changes (mutates) the data members so that the fraction becomes its own reciprocal. Mutators are usually void, and are not marked "const."

⟨Fraction *member function declarations* 5a⟩+≡
```
void invert();
```

C++ allows us to redefine the standard operators so that we can use them appropriately with newly defined class types. This is known as *operator overloading*. In the example code using Fraction, above, we used the '+' operator to add one Fraction to another. An operator in C++ is simply a special kind of function. We have the choice of implementing operators as either member or non-member functions. However, there is a slight advantage to implementing them as non-member functions: both arguments are subject to automatic conversions, so that we can write either a + 1 or 1 + a when a is a Fraction, and the single-argument constructor will invisibly convert the int constant into a Fraction.

⟨*interface for* Fraction 3b⟩+≡
```
Fraction operator + (const Fraction& a, const Fraction& b);
Fraction operator - (const Fraction& a, const Fraction& b);
Fraction operator * (const Fraction& a, const Fraction& b);
Fraction operator / (const Fraction& a, const Fraction& b);
Fraction operator - (const Fraction& a);    // unary '-'
Fraction operator + (const Fraction& a);    // unary '+'
```

Note that these declarations are placed *after* the class declaration. The phrase "const Fraction& a" is a C++ idiom. The '&' marks a as a *reference parameter*, so that a reference to a Fraction is passed rather than the value itself. The 'const' means that a is constant; its value is not changed within the function. This provides the efficiency of a reference parameter combined with the safety of a value parameter. For this reason, you should always use "const reference" parameters when passing Fraction (or any other class, including string) values to functions.

If we're going to provide the arithmetic operators, we should also provide each of the corresponding "compound assignment" operators. These must be member functions, since they make changes to the object's underlying representation.

⟨Fraction *member function declarations* 5a⟩+≡
```
Fraction& operator += (const Fraction& other);
Fraction& operator -= (const Fraction& other);
Fraction& operator *= (const Fraction& other);
Fraction& operator /= (const Fraction& other);
```

The '&' in the return type of each of these functions marks them as returning a reference to a Fraction instead of a Fraction value. Returning a reference instead of a value allows an object to be used on the left-hand side of an assignment statement. This doesn't seem very useful here, but it is traditional for assignment operators (for reasons that are not important here), and is absolutely necessary for our next declaration: the '<<' output operator.

The '<<' operation cannot be a member function, because the left-hand operand must be the stream the output is sent to, not a Fraction object. The reference return is what allows the "cout << a << b << c" construction you've been using since you first started working with C++. Once we define this operator, any of these output values can be a Fraction.

⟨*interface for* Fraction 3b⟩+≡
```
std::ostream& operator << (std::ostream& out,
                           const Fraction& f);
```

The ostream type requires the <iostream> header.

⟨#include*'s needed for* Fraction *interface* 6c⟩≡
```
#include <iostream>
```

Finally, we need to specify the relational operators:

⟨*interface for* Fraction 3b⟩+≡
```
bool operator == (const Fraction& a, const Fraction& b);
bool operator != (const Fraction& a, const Fraction& b);
bool operator <  (const Fraction& a, const Fraction& b);
bool operator <= (const Fraction& a, const Fraction& b);
bool operator >  (const Fraction& a, const Fraction& b);
bool operator >= (const Fraction& a, const Fraction& b);
```

The Implementation

The first item on the implementation agenda is to settle on a *representation*, which is embodied in the data members. It seems natural to represent a Fraction as two integers, which we'll call num and denom, for its numerator and denominator, respectively. We should always keep the representation in its "simplest terms," meaning that the numerator and denominator share no factors and only the numerator may be negative.

⟨*fraction.cpp* 7a⟩≡

```
⟨#include's needed for Fraction implementation 8b⟩
#include "fraction.h"

using namespace std;

⟨implementation of Fraction 7d⟩
```

⟨Fraction *data members and private function declarations* 7b⟩≡
```
int num, denom;
```

Once we've settled on a representation, it makes sense to implement the constructors. The primary purpose of a constructor is to initialize an object's data members. Fraction only has one constructor with two integer parameters (default arguments are listed only in the member function declaration/interface, not in its definition/implementation).

There are two ways to initialize data members: using assignment statements or *member initializer lists*. We use the latter technique, in which a colon introduces a list of data members, with their initial values in parentheses, from the function prototype. Anything more than simple initialization can be dealt with in the constructor body. For example, once we set num and denom from the parameter values, we need to make sure that the Fraction is in its simplest terms. We use a private member function, reduce, to do this.

⟨Fraction *data members and private function declarations* 7b⟩+≡
```
void reduce();
```

When defining member functions (including constructors), we must specify the function's *full name*. Otherwise, the compiler won't know to which class the function belongs. The full name of a member function is formed by using the class name with the ':::' symbol as a prefix. Thus the full name of the constructor is "Fraction::Fraction." Note that we do not repeat the default argument specifications here; they belong only in the interface declaration.

⟨*implementation of* Fraction 7d⟩≡
```
Fraction::Fraction(int n, int d) : num(n), denom(d)
{
    reduce();
}
```

To reduce a Fraction to its simplest terms, we need to ensure that the denominator is not zero (in which case we throw an *exception*—the best way of reporting errors in a C++ function). If the numerator is zero, the denominator must be one. Otherwise, we must make sure that only the numerator is negative (by negating both numerator and denominator if the latter is negative), and divide both the numerator and denominator by the greatest common divisor of their absolute values (the denominator is already positive).

⟨*implementation of* Fraction 7d⟩+≡

```
void Fraction::reduce()
{
    if (denom == 0) {
        throw range_error("Fraction cannot have "
                          "zero denominator");
    } else if (num == 0) {
        denom = 1;
    } else {
        if (denom < 0) { num = -num; denom = -denom; }
        int gcd;
        ⟨set gcd to the greatest common divisor of |num| and denom 8c⟩
        num /= gcd;
        denom /= gcd;
    }
}
```

The `range_error` type is provided by the `<stdexcept>` header.

⟨#include*'s needed for* Fraction *implementation* 8b⟩≡

```
#include <stdexcept>
```

Computing the greatest common denominator of two positive integers, *a* and *b* is a well-known algorithm:

> **while** $a \neq 0$ **do**
> $\quad c \leftarrow a$
> $\quad a \leftarrow b \bmod a$
> $\quad b \leftarrow c$
> b is the GCD

The translation into C++ is trivial. The only thing notable about this code chunk is the extra pair of braces around it. Because C++ is a *block-structured* language, the extra braces ensure that the definition of this local variable n cannot possibly interfere with any other variable named n.

⟨*set* gcd *to the greatest common divisor of* |num| *and* denom 8c⟩≡

```
    {
        int n = abs(num);
        gcd = denom;
        while ( n != 0) {
            int tmp = n;
            n = gcd % n;
            gcd = tmp;
        }
    }
```

The `<cstdlib>` header defines `abs`.

⟨#include*'s needed for* Fraction *implementation* 8b⟩+≡
```
#include <cstdlib>
```

Implementing the `numerator` and `denominator` functions is trivial. Every member function operates on a specified object. For example, if `a` is a `Fraction`, `a.numerator()` returns the numerator of that `Fraction`. Within the body of a member function, the C++ reserved word `this`* designates the object that the function is operating on ("a" in this instance). When the name of a data member appears in a member function body, it refers to `this`'s data member (`this`'s `num` and `denom` here). More on `this` later.

⟨*implementation of* Fraction 7d⟩+≡
```
int Fraction::numerator() const { return num; }
int Fraction::denominator() const { return denom; }
```
Note again the use of full function names in the definitions.

The `reciprocal` function is only a bit more complex. We use the constructor to build a `Fraction` whose numerator and denominator are reversed from this one's, and return the newly constructed `Fraction`.

⟨*implementation of* Fraction 7d⟩+≡
```
Fraction Fraction::reciprocal() const
{
    return Fraction(denom, num);
}
```

The `value` function is also straightforward. The only tricky part is that there are many ways in C++ to convert an `int` into a `double`. The simplest is to use a `double` "constructor." It's not really necessary to convert both numerator and denominator, but it is more thorough (and somewhat clearer) this way.

⟨*implementation of* Fraction 7d⟩+≡
```
double Fraction::value() const
{
    return double(num) / double(denom);
}
```

Implementing `invert` is a bit tricky because the numerator might be zero or negative. Reducing the result to its simplest terms after swapping numerator and denominator deals with these possibilities.

⟨*implementation of* Fraction 7d⟩+≡
```
void Fraction::invert()
{
    std::swap(num, denom);
    reduce();
}
```

---

*The only pronoun in C++.

The standard `swap` function is defined in the `<utility>` header for C++11 (but in `<algorithm>` before C++11).

⟨#include*'s needed for* `Fraction` *implementation* 8b⟩+≡
```
#include <utility>
```

The compound assignment operators are fairly straightforward. They perform the specified operation, reduce the result to its simplest terms, and return the current object, "`*this`" (the '`*`' will be explained later— Section 1.3).

Adding one `Fraction` to another involves finding a common denominator, and adding the corresponding numerators. The easiest way to do this is to multiply the denominators together to get a new denominator. The new numerator is computed by multiplying each operand's numerator by the denominator of the other operand and adding the results. Of course, we must reduce the `Fraction` to its simplest terms before we return.

⟨*implementation of* `Fraction` 7d⟩+≡
```
Fraction& Fraction::operator += (const Fraction& other)
{
    num = num * other.denom + other.num * denom;
    denom *= other.denom;
    reduce();
    return *this;
}
```

Subtracting one `Fraction` from another is the same as adding them, except we subtract the numerators instead of adding.

⟨*implementation of* `Fraction` 7d⟩+≡
```
Fraction& Fraction::operator -= (const Fraction& other)
{
    num = num * other.denom - other.num * denom;
    denom *= other.denom;
    reduce();
    return *this;
}
```

To multiply one `Fraction` by another, we multiply the numerators and denominators separately.

⟨*implementation of* `Fraction` 7d⟩+≡
```
Fraction& Fraction::operator *= (const Fraction& other)
{
    num *= other.num;
    denom *= other.denom;
    reduce();
    return *this;
}
```

Division involves multiplying this `Fraction` by the other's inverse.

⟨*implementation of* Fraction 7d⟩+≡
```
Fraction& Fraction::operator /= (const Fraction& other)
{
    num *= other.denom;
    denom *= other.num;
    reduce();
    return *this;
}
```

The arithmetic operators are not member functions, and so, must use only the public member functions and operators. They can all be implemented using their corresponding assignment operators.

The '+' operator can be defined in terms of '+=',

⟨*implementation of* Fraction 7d⟩+≡
```
Fraction operator + (const Fraction& a, const Fraction& b)
{
    Fraction result = a;
    result += b;
    return result;
}
```

'−' in terms of '−=',

⟨*implementation of* Fraction 7d⟩+≡
```
Fraction operator - (const Fraction& a, const Fraction& b)
{
    Fraction result = a;
    result -= b;
    return result;
}
```

and '*' and '/' in terms of '*=' and '/='.

⟨*implementation of* Fraction 7d⟩+≡
```
Fraction operator * (const Fraction& a, const Fraction& b)
{
    Fraction result = a;
    result *= b;
    return result;
}
Fraction operator / (const Fraction& a, const Fraction& b)
{
    Fraction result = a;
    result /= b;
    return result;
}
```

The unary operators are trivial. For unary '-' we simply return a `Fraction` identical to its argument, except that its numerator has the opposite sign. For unary '+' we just return a copy of the argument.

⟨*implementation of* `Fraction` 7d⟩+≡

```
Fraction operator - (const Fraction& a)
    { return Fraction(-a.numerator(), a.denominator()); }
Fraction operator + (const Fraction& a) { return a; }
```

When we output a `Fraction`, we want a string of the form *n/d*, where *n* and *d* are the numerator and denominator, respectively, unless the denominator is 1, in which case the `Fraction` is a whole number, and should be printed as such.

⟨*implementation of* `Fraction` 7d⟩+≡

```
ostream& operator << (ostream& out, const Fraction& f)
{
    out << f.numerator();
    if (f.denominator() != 1) { out << "/"
                                    << f.denominator(); }
    return out;
}
```

The `<iostream>` header provides the `ostream` type. You might recall that we already have a `#include <iostream>` in our `.h` file, so this one isn't really necessary. However, a reorganization of the code (sometimes called "refactoring") might move the declaration of the '<<' operator out of the `.h` file, which would then cause problems here. Since the standard headers all have the necessary guards to deal with multiple inclusion, there's no harm done by including it again here.

⟨`#include`*'s needed for* `Fraction` *implementation* 8b⟩+≡

```
#include <iostream>
```

Taking note of every header file that needs to be included tends to get in the way of more important explanations, so they will no longer be mentioned. The proper headers are, of course, `#include`-ed in the code on the companion disc.

Since a `Fraction` is always in its simplest terms, the equality operator simply needs to determine if both numerators and denominators are equal. The inequality operator is merely the inverse of equality.

⟨*implementation of* `Fraction` 7d⟩+≡

```
bool operator == (const Fraction& a, const Fraction& b)
{
    return a.numerator() == b.numerator()
            and a.denominator() == b.denominator();
}
```

```
bool operator != (const Fraction& a, const Fraction& b)
{
    return not (a == b);
}
```

Most relational operators can be defined in terms of the '<' and '=='
operators. Since we've just defined the latter, the former is the only one left
whose definition is less than trivial. As we did in implementing addition,
we simply multiply the denominators to get a common denominator for
comparison.

⟨*implementation of* Fraction 7d⟩+≡
```
bool operator <  (const Fraction& a, const Fraction& b)
{
    return a.numerator() * b.denominator()
            < b.numerator() * a.denominator();
}
bool operator <= (const Fraction& a, const Fraction& b)
{
    return a < b or a == b;
}
bool operator >  (const Fraction& a, const Fraction& b)
{
    return b < a;
}
bool operator >= (const Fraction& a, const Fraction& b)
{
    return not (a < b);
}
```

Loose Ends

We've gone into more detail than necessary in developing the Fraction
class in order to have complete examples of both a C++ class and of literate
programming in action. If you were able to follow the explanations and
understand the Fraction class, you shouldn't have any trouble with what
follows. If not, you might want to go over Section 1.2.1 again, perhaps
taking a look at the complete fraction.h and fraction.cpp files while
you do.

In the Fraction class we've been very careful to separate the interface
from the implementation. However much this is preferable conceptually, it
leads to some unnecessary inefficiencies. Although clarity is much more
important than efficiency here, C++ provides a simple enough way to deal
with this: *inline functions*. An inline function is one that looks and acts
like any other function, but does not generate the overhead that traditional
function calls do.

Inline functions are particularly useful for single-line functions, such as the member functions **numerator** and **denominator** as well as the relational operators. You can denote a member function as inline by placing its complete definition in the class declaration instead of just declaring its parameter and return types. For example, we might have written the following in **fraction.h**:

⟨Fraction *member function declarations* [[**alternate**]] 14a⟩≡
```
int numerator() const { return num; }
int denominator() const { return denom; }
    // ... etc. ...
```

which means we don't need to define these functions in **fraction.cpp**.

To designate a non-member function as inline, you use the **inline** keyword. This must be done in the **.h** file, not in the **.cpp**. For example, we might have written

⟨*interface for* Fraction [[**alternate**]] 14b⟩≡
```
inline bool operator ==(const Fraction& a, const Fraction& b)
{
    return a.numerator() == b.numerator()
            and a.denominator() == b.denominator();
}
inline bool operator !=(const Fraction& a, const Fraction& b)
{
    return not a == b;
}
    // ... etc. ...
```

in **fraction.h**, leaving the definitions out of **fraction.cpp**.

The major disadvantage of inline functions is that they muddy the distinction between interface and implementation, which reduces the readability of the code. Remember that most software is modified over its lifetime by programmers other than its original author. In the long run, clarity is better than small gains in efficiency. However, as long as you limit your inline functions to one or (at most) two lines of code each, you should be okay.

1.3 POINTERS AND ARRAYS

C++ is based on the C programming language, which was designed as a *systems* programming language, meaning that it provides more access to the underlying hardware than you might want in a general purpose language. The only one of these "low-level" features that concerns us here is the concept of *pointers* and how they relate to C/C++ arrays. C++ pointers are necessary for dealing with inheritance (see Section 1.4) and implementing data structures (see Section 1.7).

In C++, as in C, a pointer is the *address* of a hardware memory location. The unary '*' operator is used to *dereference* the pointer. If p is a pointer to an int, then *p is the int value that p points at (int is called p's *base type*). To accomplish this, you would use the declaration

```
int *p;
```

which, technically, means "*p is an int," although it is usually translated as "p is a pointer to an int," which leads some programmers to prefer to place the '*' immediately after the type name instead of just before the variable name. If this is your preference, you need to be careful. The declaration

```
int* p, q;
```

does not mean "p and q are both int pointers," but rather "*p and q are both int's," which is not the same thing. Hereafter, we keep the '*' with the variable name.

Pointer values are usually represented as arrows. If we assign the value 3 to the int pointed to by p,

```
*p = 3;
```

the result would look something like this:

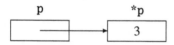

This leads to the question of how p gets a location to point to in the first place. Of course, it's always possible to assign the value of one pointer variable to another (assuming they have the same base type), but that still leaves the problem of how the first pointer variable gets its value. The C++ keyword new is used to allocate space for pointer variables. The declaration

```
int *p = new int;
```

creates the pointer variable p and initializes it to point to an (uninitialized) area of memory big enough to hold an integer value:

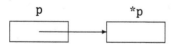

It is possible to assign a pointer a value that indicates that there is nothing being pointed to. This is called the *null pointer*, and in C++11 is designated by the keyword nullptr. Previous to C++11, the integer value zero is automatically converted to a null pointer value when required.

```
p = nullptr;    // in C++11
p = 0;          // previous to C++11
```

A null pointer value is usually drawn as a line through the box representing the pointer variable.

The dot notation for function calls can get somewhat cumbersome when used with pointers. For example, if you declare sp to be a pointer to a string:

```
string *sp;
```

you would have to use (*sp).length() to refer the length of the string pointed to by sp (the parentheses are necessary because of C++'s precedence rules). Fortunately, C++ provides a "shorthand" for saying the same thing: the expression sp->length() is equivalent to (*sp).length().

A pointer can point to a group of values. For example, the following declaration

```
int *q = new int[5];
```

initializes q to point to the first of 5 int locations:

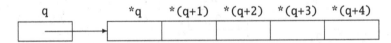

In C++, when you add an integer, n, to a pointer value, you get the address of the location n values away. Thus, *(q+1) refers to the second value pointed to by q, *(q+2) refers to the third value, and so on. This notation is somewhat cumbersome, so C++ provides the notation q[1] for *(q+1), q[2] for *(q+2), and so on (including q[0] as a synonym for *q). In other words, C++ pointers and arrays are pretty much the same things. The declaration

```
int a[10];
```

is roughly equivalent to the declaration

```
int *a = new int[10];
```

which means that you can use an array name or pointer to iterate through the multiple items referred to. Instead of

```
for (auto i = 0; i < 10; i++) {
    ⟨do something with a[i]⟩
}
```

you can write

```
for (auto ap = a; ap < a + 10; ap++) {
    ⟨do something with *ap⟩
}
```

This doesn't seem like much of an improvement (if, indeed, it is an improvement), but it will when we start dealing with iterators (Section 1.6.2).

When you no longer need the memory accessed through a pointer variable you should release it so that it may be reused. The C++ keyword delete is used to release memory when it is no longer needed. A single location (such as *p) can be released by a statement such as

```
delete p;
```

and a group of locations (such as *q and the four locations that follow it) can be released by a statement such as

```
delete[] q;
```

After these delete statements have been executed, *p and *q are no longer valid.

A program that continually uses new to allocate memory, but never uses delete to free it up when it's no longer needed, is said to have *memory leaks*. In small programs that only run for a short time, this is not usually a problem, but large programs that do a lot of computation may become unusable because of memory leaks, since needed memory is no longer accessible even though it is no longer in use.

The keyword this is actually a pointer to the current object, rather than the object itself, which explains why the compound assignment and '<<' operator functions return *this instead of just this in Section 1.2.1. Some folks prefer to use this explicitly instead of implicitly in their member function definitions. For example, we could have used this->num or this->reduce() in our Fraction member functions in place of num and reduce(). This is simply a matter of preference; C++ compilers generate the exact same code for both versions. Whichever form you prefer, be consistent. It is arguable which one is easier to understand, but a mixture of both is worse than either.

1.4 INHERITANCE

Inheritance is the feature that gives object-oriented programming its real power. The standard C++ library does not make any use of inheritance, nor do we in this book (except for the programming exercise in Chapter 6). However, it is such an important concept that it's worth covering anyway.

Inheritance is used to implement the *is-a* relationship between types. For example, you could say that every cat is a mammal and every mammal is an animal. In programming terms, this means that a `Cat` class would inherit from a `Mammal` class, which would inherit from an `Animal` class.

Another relationship between types is the *has-a* relationship, which is implemented in C++ by the data members in a class. In our `Fraction` example (Section 1.2.1), we might say

> Every fraction has a num[erator] (`int`) and denom[inator] (`int`).

which explains `Figure`'s `num` and `denom` data members.

And finally, there is the *can* relationship, which describes the operations that can be performed on a specified type. For example,

> Every fraction can be added to another fraction.
> Every fraction can be inverted.
> Every fraction can be reported as a `double` value.

The best way to explain inheritance is with an example. A traditional one, which demonstrates all the features of inheritance is that of geometrical figures. A view of the is-a relationships between (a limited number of) figure types can be expressed by the following diagram:

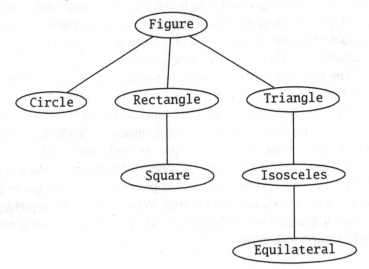

which means in English:

> Every `Circle` is a `Figure`.
> Every `Rectangle` is a `Figure`.
> Every `Square` is a `Rectangle`.
> Every `Triangle` is a `Figure`.

Every `Isosceles` is a `Triangle`.
Every `Equilateral` is an `Isosceles`.

The following discussion is limited to the types `Figure`, `Circle`, `Rectangle`, and `Square`; you should be able to flesh out the other definitions yourself. It's also limited to a small number of member functions, just enough to illustrate the necessary concepts. Please assume the existence of a `Point` class with a default constructor and a

```
void move(double dx, double dy);
```

member function.

    `Figure` is an *abstract* class, which means that not all of its member functions are implemented; one or more must be supplied by the classes that inherit from it. (In this instance, `Figure` is called the *base class* and the inherited classes are called *derived classes*.) We know the following about the `Figure` class:

Every `Figure` has a location (`Point`).
Every `Figure` can move by Δx, Δy.
Every `Figure` can compute its area.

    The first statement gives us a data member:

⟨`Figure` *data members and private function declarations* 19a⟩≡
```
Point location;
```

and constructor

⟨`Figure` *constructor declarations* 19b⟩≡
```
Figure(const Point& p = Point()) : location(p) {}
```

that needs only to intialize `location`.

    To move a figure by Δx, Δy, we only have to move its `location`.

⟨`Figure` *member function declarations* 19c⟩≡
```
void move(double dx, double dy) { location.move(dx, dy); }
```

    The `compute_area` function, however is a different kettle of fish. Even though every `Figure` can compute its area, the formulas for each of these is different. In C++, we use the "= 0" notation to indicate that a member function must be implemented in the derived classes. Such functions are called *pure virtual* member functions.

⟨`Figure` *member function declarations* 19c⟩+≡
```
virtual double compute_area() const = 0;
```

The `virtual` keyword means that we intend to *override* the definition of `compute_area` in classes derived from `Figure`. Any member function (even those that are not "pure") may be marked as `virtual`. In that case, the base class implementation will be the default implementation for any derived class that chooses not to override it. For example, we could have declared **Figure::move** to be **virtual**, but there isn't any advantage in doing so.

We know the following about the **Circle** class:

Every **Circle** is a **Figure**.
Every **Circle** has a radius (**double**).
Every **Circle** can compute its area.

Every **Circle** can, of course, move too, but the fact that every **Circle** is a **Figure** takes care of that. In other words, **Circle** *inherits* move from **Figure**. We indicate this with a colon, the keyword **public**, and the name of the base class in the derived class declaration:

⟨*interface for* Circle 20a⟩≡
```
class Circle : public Figure {
public:
    ⟨Circle constructor declarations 20c⟩
    ⟨Circle member function declarations 20d⟩
private:
    ⟨Circle data members and private function declarations 20b⟩
};
```
We can see that **Circle** has one data member, **radius**, in addition to **location**, which is inherited from **Figure**.

⟨Circle *data members and private function declarations* 20b⟩≡
```
double radius;
```
The **Circle** constructor initializes the former directly, and uses the **Figure** constructor to initialize the latter. Default arguments select the default **Point** value if no location is specified, and a unit circle if no radius is specified as well.

⟨Circle *constructor declarations* 20c⟩≡
```
Circle(double r = 1.0, const Point& p = Point())
    : Figure(p), radius(r) {}
```
As everyone knows, the formula for the area of a circle is πr^2.

⟨Circle *member function declarations* 20d⟩≡
```
double compute_area() const
    { return M_PI * radius * radius; }
```
There is no need to use the **virtual** keyword again in the derived class, although you may if you want to. Some programmers prefer to restate **virtual** wherever possible; others prefer not to.

The **Rectangle** class is similar to the **Circle** class,

Every **Rectangle** is a **Figure**.
Every **Rectangle** has a width (**double**) and a height (**double**).
Every **Rectangle** can compute its area.

with `width` and `height` rather than `radius`, and no default values for either of these in the constructor. So the complete class definition looks like this:

⟨*interface for* Rectangle 21a⟩≡
```
class Rectangle : public Figure {
public:
    Rectangle(double w, double h, const Point& p = Point())
        : Figure(p), width(w), height(h) {}
    double compute_area() const { return width * height; }
private:
    double width, height;
};
```

A `Square` inherits everything it needs from `Rectangle`; the only difference is that its `width` and `length` are equal, so a constructor is the only thing we need to define.

⟨*interface for* Square 21b⟩≡
```
class Square : public Rectangle {
public:
    Square(double w, const Point& p = Point())
        : Rectangle(w, w, p) {}
};
```

The power of inheritance comes from what is called *polymorphism*, which means that each object in a derived class knows what it is and performs the appropriate operation, even if the type of its variable is of the class's base type. In C++, this works only with pointers.* For example, if `f` is a pointer to a figure,

```
Figure *f;
```

you can assign it to point to a value of any type derived from `Figure`. All the following assignment statements are legal in C++:

```
f = new Circle(3);
f = new Square(10);
f = new Rectangle(4, 5);
```

and `f->compute_area()` will use the appropriate computation, depending on what kind of figure `f` actually points to (returning 28.27436, 100, and 20, respectively for the above examples).

If you have an array of `Figure` pointers, you can use this to compute the combined area of all the figures in the array,

---

*Actually, there's no absolute requirement that you use pointers, but if you don't, things won't always work the way you think they should.

```
Figure *figs[] = {
    new Circle(), new Circle(10),
    new Rectangle(3, 5), new Square(7:
};
double total_area = 0;
for (auto i = 0; i < 4; i++)
{
    total_area += f[i]->compute_area();
}
cout << "total area is " << total_area << endl;
```

1.5 TEMPLATES

Very often we come across an algorithm that is independent of the type of data involved. For example, a simple technique for finding the position of *item* in an n-element array, a, returning -1 if the value is not found, is to check each element in a in order until the value is found or every element has been checked:

> **for** i **from** 0 **to** $n - 1$ **do**
>   **if** $a[i] = item$ **then**
>   return i
> return -1

It makes no difference what type of elements are contained in the array; the algorithm is the same. It would be nice to be able to write a single *generic* function that would work with int arrays, double arrays, string arrays, and so on.

To allow this, C++ provides the *template* concept. Like its name suggests, a template is pattern for a function to be generated by the compiler when it is needed. Using templates, we can write a lookup function to implement the above algorithm:

```
template<typename T>
int lookup(const T& item, T a[], int n)
{
    for (auto i = 0; i < n; i++) {
        if (a[i] == item) { return i; }
    }
    return -1;
}
```

The template header specifies that within the following definition the identifier "T" is a placeholder for the name of a type. We can now write code like the following:

```
int a1[];
double a2[];
int n1, n2;        // no. of elements in a1 and a2, respectively
   ⋮
... lookup(6, a1, n1) ...
... lookup(7.3, a2, n2) ...
```

The C++ compiler uses function arguments to infer what T is in each lookup call, whenever possible. However, there are occasions when this is not possible, when you have to specify the template parameter explicitly. For example, if n3 contains the length of a string array, a3, the call

```
... lookup("hello", a3, n3) ...
```

generates a compilation error, which can be avoided by specifying <string> as the template parameter in the function call:

```
... lookup<string>("hello", a3, n3) ...
```

Classes as well as functions can be defined as templates. In fact, all of the remaining classes defined in this book are defined as templates (so an example here would be superfluous). Because templates are patterns for generating code rather than actual code, they belong in .h rather than .cpp files.

1.6 THE STANDARD TEMPLATE LIBRARY (STL)

The Standard Template Library (STL) is the part of the standard C++ library that deals with traditional data structures. To understand the STL, there are three concepts to deal with: *containers*, *iterators*, and *algorithms*.

1.6.1 Containers

Each data structure provided by the STL is a *container*: a collection of values of some type organized in some way. Each container class organizes its data differently, but uses similar names for similar operations. Although the STL doesn't provide a class named "container," the following explanations are simpler if we use container as a substitute for the name of any STL container class. Each container class is provided by a header file named for the class: <vector>, <list>, <stack>, <queue>, and so on.

As its name implies, the STL provides template classes. The `container` class would be defined as something like this:

```
template <typename T>
class container {
public:
    ⟨container constructor declarations⟩
    ⟨container member function declarations⟩
private:
    ⟨container data members and private function declarations⟩
};
```

Every container class provides a default constructor that creates an empty container, and the accessors `size` and `empty`, which respectively, report on the number of elements in the container and whether or not that value is zero, and `empty` can safely be defined in terms of `size`.

⟨container *constructor declarations*⟩≡
```
container();
```

⟨container *member function declarations*⟩≡
```
int size() const;
bool empty() const { return size() == 0; }
```

They also provide insertion and removal functions, which are usually (but not always) named with some variation of "**push**" and "**pop**," respectively.

⟨container *member function declarations*⟩+≡
```
void push(const T& item);
void pop();
```

Since **pop** does not return a value, STL containers also provide one or more functions that provide access to a single element in the container. The names of these functions vary widely, and depend on the organization of data in the container. Sometimes they have parameters, sometimes not.

⟨container *member function declarations*⟩+≡
```
T& element();
```

The following code illustrates the use of these functions. The value printed by the second `cout` depends, of course, on how **element** is defined.

```
container<int> c;          // construct an empty container
c.push(-3);                // insert a couple of values
c.push(77);
cout << c.size();          // will print 2
cout << c.element();       // will print -3 or 77
c.pop();                   // remove one of the elements
cout << c.size();          // will print 1
```

1.6.2 Iterators

Most (but not all) of the container types defined in the STL provide *iterators* for the container. An iterator is a value that mimics a pointer and allows you to access the elements in the container in some kind of order. Each iterator type defines at least the unary '*' (dereference)*, '!=' (not equal) and '++' (increment operators), and is usually given the alias "iterator" within the container class. A container class with iterators cooperates by providing member functions named "begin" and "end" that return iterators denoting the beginning and end of the iteration:

⟨container *member function declarations*⟩+≡
```
    typedef ⟨actual iterator type name⟩ iterator;
    iterator begin();
    iterator end();
```

Using **begin** and **end**, you can cycle through the elements of our example container, c, with the following C++ code:

```
    for (auto p = c.begin(); p != c.end(); p++) {
        ⟨do something with *p⟩
    }
```

which demonstrates the advantage of the C++11 definition of auto. Without auto, you would have have to write

```
    for (container<int>::iterator p = c.begin();
                            p != c.end(); p++) {
        ⟨do something with *p⟩
    }
```

which is more complicated and harder to understand. Note that the end iterator refers to a position *after* the last element, not to the last element itself.

1.6.3 Algorithms

The STL also provides template functions that implement useful algorithms on containers, which may be accessed by #include-ing the <algorithm> header. These functions operate using iterator types (which generously includes pointers, so these functions work equally well on arrays). The only two used in this book are

```
    template <typename Src, typename Dest>
    void copy(Src::iterator begin, Src::iterator end,
            Dest::iterator d_begin);
```

---

*It's usually a good idea to define the '->' (structure pointer dereference) operator, as well.

which copies elements from the source container to the destination container (if there is not enough space in the destination container, the results are undefined), and

```
template <typename Iter, typename T>
void fill(Iter begin, Iter end, const T& value);
```

which fills the range specified by the iterators with the given value.

Some of the other <algorithm> functions require more sophisticated iterator types than those described here. They aren't used in this book, but you're welcome to explore them (and any changes you'll need to make in our iterator class definitions) on your own.

1.7 PUTTING IT ALL TOGETHER: A VECTOR CLASS

The first STL container class most programmers encounter is the vector class, which provides something of a replacement for arrays. Unlike an array, a vector can report on the number of elements it contains and can expand and shrink as needed. All STL containers provide the member functions size and empty (which report on the number of elements contained), and most also provide the iterator functions begin and end, plus the clear function (which empties the container). The vector class provides all of these, plus the following:

Accessors

capacity	current allocation size
front	first element
back	last element
operator[]	specified element
at	specified element (w/ range check)

Mutators

push_back	add an element to the end
pop_back	remove the last element
resize	change the number of elements stored

Our implementation is called "`Vector`" to distinguish it from the standard version. It is a template class, which is declared similarly to a template function,

⟨*interface for* `Vector` 27a⟩≡
```
template <typename T>
class Vector {
public:
        ⟨Vector constructor declarations 27c⟩
        ⟨Vector member function declarations 28c⟩
private:
        ⟨Vector data members and private function declarations 27b⟩
};
```

To implement a `Vector`, we'll use a pointer/array (`data`), a count of the number of elements that space is allocated for (`allocated`), and a count of the number of elements actually in use (`used`).

⟨`Vector` *data members and private function declarations* 27b⟩≡
```
T *data;
int allocated, used;
```

1.7.1 Constructors/Destructors

The basic constructor specifies the number of elements in the vector and the value to initialize each element to, with default parameters that give us a default constructor that creates an empty `Vector` and a single-parameter constructor that specifies the number of default-valued elements. If the number of elements requested is less than zero, we change it to zero, since a container can never have fewer than zero elements.

⟨`Vector` *constructor declarations* 27c⟩≡
```
Vector(int num_elements = 0, const T& init = T())
{
        used = allocated = std::max(num_elements, 0);
        ⟨allocate space for allocated elements in data 27d⟩
        ⟨initialize the elements of data to init 27e⟩
}
```

⟨*allocate space for* `allocated` *elements in* `data` 27d⟩≡
```
data = new T[allocated];
```

The STL's `fill` function takes care of the initialization.

⟨*initialize the elements of* `data` *to* `init` 27e⟩≡
```
std::fill(data, data + used, init);
```

Whenever you implement a class that allocates space for one or more data members using **new**, you need to implement a *destructor* that releases that space when a variable of that type is destroyed (to prevent inadvertent memory leaks). A destructor is named by prefixing a tilde ('~') to the class name. If the class is to be inherited from (which is not the case here), the destructor should be declared to be `virtual`.

Our destructor simply uses `delete[]` to release the space allocated to `data`:

⟨Vector *constructor declarations* 27c⟩+≡
```
~Vector() { delete[] data; }
```

When we use pointer data members, we also need to define a *copy constructor* (to construct a `Vector` from an already existing one),

⟨Vector *constructor declarations* 27c⟩+≡
```
Vector(const Vector<T>& other)
{
    allocated = other.allocated;
    used = other.used;
```
⟨*allocate space for* `allocated` *elements in* `data` 27d⟩
⟨*initialize the elements of* `data` *to those of* `other` 28d⟩
```
}
```

and an *assignment operator* (to assign the value of one `Vector` to another).

⟨Vector *member function declarations* 28c⟩≡
```
Vector<T>& operator = (const Vector<T>& other)
{
    if (this != &other) {    // ignore assignment to self
        delete[] data;
        allocated = other.allocated;
        used = other.used;
```
⟨*allocate space for* `allocated` *elements in* `data` 27d⟩
⟨*initialize the elements of* `data` *to those of* `other` 28d⟩
```
    }
    return *this;
}
```

The unary '&' operator (which is highly dangerous, and rarely needed) gives the machine address of (in other words, a pointer to) its operand. If the pointer `this` is equal to the address of `other` in an assignment, then an attempt is being made to assign a `Vector` to itself, which can be ignored.

The STL's `copy` function can easily duplicate elements from the `other` `Vector` in our copy constructor and assignment operator implementation.

⟨*initialize the elements of* `data` *to those of* `other` 28d⟩≡
```
std::copy(other.data, other.data + other.used, data);
```

C++11 provides an `initializer_list<T>` type (defined in the <initializer_list> header), which allows initializations of the form

```
Vector<int> v = {1, 2, 3};
```

for programmer-defined types like `Vector`. All we need is a constructor that takes an `initializer_list<T>` as a parameter, and uses `copy` and an `initializer_list` iterator to put its values into `data`.

⟨Vector *constructor declarations* 27c⟩+≡
```
Vector(std::initializer_list<T> init)
{
    used = allocated = init.size();
    ⟨allocate space for allocated elements in data 27d⟩
    std::copy(init.begin(), init.end(), data);
}
```

1.7.2 Member Functions

Accessors

The easiest member function to implement is empty, as we can use the "universal" definition: `return size() == 0`; a Vector is empty if and only if its size is zero.

⟨Vector *member function declarations* 28c⟩+≡
```
bool empty() const { return size() == 0; }
```

Almost equally easy to implement are the accessors size and capacity, since they merely return the values of the corresponding data members used and allocated.

⟨Vector *member function declarations* 28c⟩+≡
```
int size() const { return used; }
int capacity() const { return allocated; }
```

The ways of const are many and strange, but when you dig deeply, you will find that they usually make good sense. However, we do not have the time (or the need) here to dig deeply. Suffice it to say (for now) that member functions that return references into an object should never be declared const, but should also have a corresponding const member function that returns a const reference. Thus it is with the '[]' operator, which must return a reference to a specific data element so that it can be used on the left-hand size of an assignment statement:

```
v[i] = ···
```

We need both const and non-const versions, returning the element of the data array specified by the given index.

⟨Vector *member function declarations* 28c⟩+≡
```
      T& operator[](int index)       { return data[index]; }
const T& operator[](int index) const { return data[index]; }
```

The same holds true for front and back, which are really only specialized versions of '[]', returning the first and last element, respectively.

⟨Vector *member function declarations* 28c⟩+≡
```
      T& front()       { return data[0]; }
      T& back()        { return data[used - 1]; }
const T& front() const { return data[0]; }
const T& back()  const { return data[used - 1]; }
```

In our `Vector` implementation, as in an STL `vector`, `front` and `back` assume that the `Vector` is not empty, and the '`[]`' operator assumes that the index is valid. If these assumptions are not correct, our code (and the STL's) behaves unpredictably. To deal with this problem, the STL `vector` class provides the `at` member function, which works exactly like '`[]`', except that it throws an `out_of_range` exception when the index is invalid. Again we need duplicate `const` and non-`const` versions.

⟨Vector *member function declarations* 28c⟩+≡
```
  T& at(int index)
  {
      if (index < 0 or index >= used) {
          throw std::out_of_range("Vector index out of range");
      }
      return data[index];
  }
  const T& at(int index) const
  {
      if (index < 0 or index >= used) {
          throw std::out_of_range("Vector index out of range");
      }
      return data[index];
  }
```

Mutators

To implement **push_back**, we have to resize the `Vector` so that it holds (at least) one more element, and place the specified value in the new last location, specified by the new value of `used` (as adjusted by `resize`).

⟨Vector *member function declarations* 28c⟩+≡
```
  void push_back(const T& value)
  {
      resize(used + 1);          // Note: resize changes used
      data[used - 1] = value;
  }
```

Implementing **pop_back** is equally simple. To be compatible with an STL `vector`, all we have to do is to decrement `used`, but allowing `used` to go negative is bad programming practice, so our version for `Vector` only decrements when this won't happen.

⟨Vector *member function declarations* 28c⟩+≡
```
  void pop_back() { if (used > 0) { --used; } }
```

To clear a `Vector`, we merely set `used` (which keeps track of the `Vector`'s size) to zero. The `Vector`'s capacity, of course, remains the same.

⟨Vector *member function declarations* 28c⟩+≡
```
  void clear() { used = 0; }
```

The last, and trickiest of the `Vector` mutators is `resize`, as it may involve allocating more space for `data` (when the new size is larger than the current capacity). If the new size is larger than the old size, the new elements must be initialized to its type's default value or a value specified by parameter. The `Vector`'s size (represented by the `used` data member) is adjusted accordingly.

⟨`Vector` *member function declarations* 28c⟩+≡
```
void resize(int new_size, const T& init = T())
{
    ⟨allocate more space for data, if necessary 31b⟩
    ⟨initialize any new elements of data to init 31d⟩
    used = new_size;
}
```

When we allocate more space for `data`, we need to copy all the values from the old area to the new one. If we simply expand the `Vector`'s capacity to its new size each time, successive calls to `push_back` will each result in a new allocation and copying of data. Since this is extremely wasteful (and needlessly slow), we need to find a better way to allocate space whenever a `Vector` needs more capacity. A technique that seems to work well in practice is to double the existing capacity whenever we need to expand `data` (unless, of course, the requested size is larger than that).

⟨*allocate more space for* `data`, *if necessary* 31b⟩≡
```
if (new_size > allocated) {
    T *old_data = data;
    allocated = std::max(new_size, 2 * allocated);
    ⟨allocate space for allocated elements in data 27d⟩
    ⟨copy values from old_data to the new data 31c⟩
    delete[] old_data;
}
```

Copying values from the old array to the new one is a straightforward use of the `copy` function,

⟨*copy values from* `old_data` *to the new* `data` 31c⟩≡
```
std::copy(old_data, old_data + used, data);
```

and initializing any new elements is a straightforward use of `fill`.

⟨*initialize any new elements of* `data` *to* `init` 31d⟩≡
```
if (new_size > used) {
    std::fill(data + used, data + new_size, init);
}
```

1.7.3 Iterators

Since a `Vector`'s elements are all contained in the `data` array, and C++ iterators are designed to look and act like pointers, we use a pointer into that array to implement an iterator. A `typedef` declaration allows us to provide `Vector::iterator` as an alias for "pointer to `T`."

⟨Vector *member function declarations* 28c⟩+≡
```
typedef T *iterator;
iterator begin() { return data; }
iterator    end() { return data + used; }
```

As with the indexing operations, iterators need to deal with `const` issues. This is traditionally done by defining a "`const_iterator`" type to provide iterators for `const` objects.

⟨Vector *member function declarations* 28c⟩+≡
```
typedef const T *const_iterator;
const_iterator begin() const { return data; }
const_iterator    end() const { return data + used; }
```

PROGRAMMING EXERCISE

Early programming languages (such as Algol) and later ones (such as Pascal and Ada) let programmers specify both lower and upper bounds for array indexes; the lower bound was not fixed at zero. Define an `Array` class that provides all the functions of `Vector`, but whose constructor

```
Array(int lower = 1, upper = 0, const T& init = T());
```

specifies both the upper and lower index bounds. Additional accessor functions **lwb** and **upb** should return the `Array`'s lower and upper index bounds, respectively.

CHAPTER 2

ALGORITHM ANALYSIS

W hether or not you remember, you have almost certainly already been introduced to the idea of an *algorithm*. Simply put, an algorithm is an unambiguous step-by-step description of a process. A C++ program is simply a formal representation of an algorithm written in the C++ programming language. Because there are many different programming languages, programmers usually write (and develop and discuss) algorithms in English (or some other human language) and then translate them into C++ (or some other programming language).

As soon as you start developing algorithms, you run up against the question of how good they are. Sometimes you may think of two or more algorithms that solve the same problem, and you need a way to determine which of the algorithms is the best one to use. You could, of course, program them all in C++ and run the programs to see how fast they are and how much memory they use, but that would take a lot of work, especially when you consider the time needed for testing and debugging.

That's where *algorithm analysis* comes in. It allows you to estimate each algorithm's requirements in terms of both memory space and running time without actually having to write (and test and debug) any code. Most of the time we are concerned with an algorithm's running time rather than its memory requirements, so unless otherwise specified, run-time rather than space efficiency is being referred to.

Since the running time of a program depends on so many different factors (programming language, compiler optimizations, processor speed, and so on), we need a way to determine an algorithm's efficiency without actually running a program. We do this by counting the number of operations performed when the algorithm is executed.

For example, you have almost certainly already seen the algorithm for computing the average value in an *n*-element array, *a* ($n \neq 0$):

> *sum* ← 0
> **for** *i* **from** 0 **to** $n - 1$ **do**
>   *sum* ← *sum* + *a*[*i*]
> *average* ← $\frac{sum}{n}$

The first assignment statement is a single operation; each of the other assignments has two operations (an addition or division along with the assignment). The loop executes its body *n* times (once for each value of *i* from 0 through $n - 1$). The key word here is *times*, which indicates multiplication. Thus, the loop executes $n \times 2$ operations, and the entire algorithm executes $1 + n \times 2 + 2 = 2n + 3$ operations.

Another, slightly more complex example is the multiplication of two $n \times n$ matrices, *a* and *b*, producing the $n \times n$ matrix *result*:

> **for** *i* **from** 0 **to** $n - 1$ **do**
>   **for** *j* **from** 0 **to** $n - 1$ **do**
>   *sum* ← 0
>   **for** *k* **from** 0 **to** $n - 1$ **do**
>   *sum* ← *sum* + *a*[*i*][*k*] × *b*[*k*][*j*]
>   *result*[*i*][*j*] ← *sum*
> **return** *result*

Each of the loops executes its body *n* times; the innermost assignment statement consists of three operations; the other two assignments are single operations; and the return statement is a single operation. The entire algorithm, therefore, executes $n \times (n \times (1 + n \times 3 + 1)) + 1 = 3n^3 + 2n^2 + 1$ operations. If you think of subscripting as an independent operation, the result would be $n \times (n \times (1 + n \times 7 + 3)) + 1 = 7n^3 + 4n^2 + 1$ operations, which is not significantly different, as you will see.

2.1 BIG-O NOTATION

There are many notations, such as big-Ω and big-Θ, related to algorithm analysis, each of which has a precise mathematical meaning, but for our purposes, it's simpler to lump them all together into a single notation. *Big-O notation* relates the efficiency of an algorithm to some function of *n*, where *n* is usually the number of elements in a collection. For example, if an algorithm is $O(n)$, it means that the running time of the algorithm is roughly proportional to the number of elements in the collection. Big-O actually has a more precise mathematical meaning, but this is good enough. It may help to think that the 'O' in big-O stands for "On the Order Of."

To determine the big-O efficiency of an algorithm, you simply take the function describing the number of operations executed (in terms of *n*), reduce all coefficients to one, and remove all the terms except the most significant one. In this way, the efficiency of the average-computing and matrix multiplication algorithms can be described as $O(n)$ and $O(n^3)$, respectively.

2.1.1 Terminology

Constant Time

Code that takes roughly the same amount of time to execute, regardless of the value of n is said to be $O(1)$; to run in *constant time*. Since all coefficients reduce to one in big-O computations, the earlier subscripting operations don't matter. In fact, you don't really need to consider the arithmetic operations as separate, either. All simple statements in an algorithm, except for function calls, are considered single operations as far as big-O is concerned. In fact, any sequence of consecutive simple statements is $O(1)$, and can be treated as a single operation.

Linear Time

Algorithms that are $O(n)$ are said to run in *linear time*. An interesting example is a simple search through an n-element array, a, to find the location of a given value, x, returning -1 if it's not there:

```
for i from 0 to n − 1 do
    if a[i] = x then
        return i
return −1
```

This algorithm is known as *linear search*. What makes it interesting is that the loop doesn't always execute n times. If the value x is in $a[0]$, it only executes once. If the value is not in the array at all, it makes the full n iterations, but if x is found, the loop terminates early. Thus, linear search has a *best case*, a *worst case*, and an *average case*. The best case, when the search value is in the first element, is $O(1)$. The worst case, when the value is not in the array, is $O(n)$. On average, however, the loop will end up looking halfway through the array to find a value, using $\frac{n}{2}$ iterations, which is also $O(n)$ (remember that all coefficients reduce to one when doing big-O analysis).

Quadratic Time

A $O(n^2)$ algorithm is said to run in *quadratic time*. A classic example of a $O(n^2)$ algorithm is *bubble sort*, which rearranges the elements of an n-element array, a, in order from the smallest to the largest:

```
for i from 0 to n − 2 do
    for j from 0 to n − 2 − i do
        if a[j + 1] < a[j] then
            swap the values of a[j + 1] and a[j]
```

The iterations of the inner loop depend on the value of i in the current iteration of the outer loop. The first time the inner loop runs it executes its body $n − 1$ times ($n − 2 − 0$ plus 1 because the count starts at zero), the second $n − 2$ times, and so on, down to one (from zero to zero). Since it takes constant time to check a condition and to swap two values, the total number of operations is $(n − 1) + (n − 2) + \cdots + 2 + 1$, which (by a well-known formula) is equal to $\frac{n(n−1)}{2} = \frac{1}{2}n^2 − \frac{1}{2}n$, which is $O(n^2)$.

Quadratic time is a special case of *polynomial time*, $O(n^k)$, where k is a constant. Another special case is $O(n^3)$, which is called *cubic time*.

Logarithmic Time

Many algorithms involve a strategy called "divide and conquer." A good example of this is *binary search*, which like linear search finds the location of a given value, x, in an n-element array, a, returning $−1$ if the value is not in the array. However, the binary search algorithm requires that the elements of the array be in order, with $a[0] \leq a[1] \leq \cdots \leq a[n−1]$ (Figure 2.1). The

FIGURE 2.1 Array with elements in order, for binary search

algorithm starts by "probing" the middle element of the whole array. If that value is too small or too large, the range to search is redefined, depending on which half of the array the value must be in, and the process is repeated for the new, shorter range. If, at any time, the value is found in a middle element or the size of the range shrinks to zero, the algorithm terminates. This is much like a number guessing game where the guesser is told only "higher," "lower," or "correct."

```
lower ← 0
upper ← n − 1
while lower ≤ upper do
    mid ← (lower + upper) ÷ 2    // '÷' stands for integer division
    if a[mid] = x then
        return mid
    else if a[mid] < x then
        lower ← mid + 1
    else    // a[mid] > x
        upper ← mid − 1
return −1
```

Since each probe divides the search space in half, there can be at most $\lceil \log_2 n \rceil$ probes before the value is found or the search space is exhausted. On average, half this number of probes will be necessary. Binary search is therefore $O(\log n)$.

Exponential Time

Some algorithms run in *exponential time*; they are $O(k^n)$, where k is some constant, usually 2. An example of an exponential algorithm is one that prints every possible n-letter combination. Since there are 26^n possible n-letter combinations in English, any such algorithm would be $O(26^n)$.

2.2 EFFICIENCY OF VECTOR OPERATIONS

Now is a good time to take a look at the efficiency of the member functions in our Vector class (Section 1.7). The size, capacity, front, back, clear, pop_back, begin and end functions, and the '[]' operator are all implemented with single, simple statements, and are therefore all $O(1)$, as is the destructor. The empty function invokes size in a simple statement, but since size is $O(1)$, empty is too. The at function is the same as the '[]' operator with an extra if, so it too is $O(1)$.

All of the constructors and the assignment operator are $O(n)$. Allocating space is a constant time operation, but the standard functions fill and copy, which initialize the space, iterate through all n elements, which means that the constructors must be $O(n)$.

The resize function also uses fill to initialize part of the data area. Sometimes resize is used to make a Vector smaller, in which case no initialization is necessary. However, when the Vector is expanded, the new elements must be initialized, and when it is necessary to allocate more space, the entire contents must be copied to the new area. If we assume that most of the time resize will be used to expand a Vector, then on average, at least some fraction of the data area will be initialized, which means that resize is $O(n)$, whether or not data needs to be copied.

The most interesting of the Vector functions, from an algorithm analysis point of view, is push_back. Because push_back invokes resize, which is $O(n)$, before assigning a value to a new data element, you might think that it must also be $O(n)$. However, this is not actually the case. You need to look at how resize's implementation interacts with its use. Each time resize is called by push_back, it only asks for a single new element. If the Vector already has sufficient capacity for the new element, you get resize's best case behavior, which is $O(1)$. If not, it will double the Vector's capacity, which will necessitate copying the old contents (which is a $O(n)$ operation) and initializing a single element (which is $O(1)$). However, since `resize` doubles the `Vector`'s capacity only when it needs to allocate more space, these allocations will be relatively rare, which makes the time for copying relatively insignificant. In the long run, the efficiency of `push_back` approaches $O(1)$. This is what is known as *amortized* efficiency.

Since `Vector` uses simple pointers for iterators, all the iterator operations are $O(1)$. In fact, the iterator operations (including `begin` and `end`) for all STL iterators run in constant time.

In terms of space efficiency, a `Vector` allocates space for, at most, $2n - 1$ elements, which of course is $O(n)$. If the elements themselves are large, however, this may involve a lot of wasted space.

2.3 ESTIMATES AND COMPARISONS

Assume that a $O(n^2)$ algorithm takes about 1 second to process 1,000 elements. About how long will it take to process 100,000 elements? Since big-O relates running time to the number of operations performed, we get the following approximation:

$$\frac{1 \text{ sec}}{1,000^2 \text{ operations}} \approx \frac{x \text{ sec}}{100,000^2 \text{ operations}},$$

which, after cross-multiplying, gives

$$1,000^2 x \approx 100,000^2 = 100^2 \times 1,000^2$$
$$x \approx 100^2 = 10,000 \text{ sec.}$$

10,000 seconds is pretty meaningless, but we can divide by 60 to get the number of minutes, and then by 60 again to get the number of hours. The bad news is that 60 doesn't divide 10,000 evenly, but the good news is that this is only an estimate, so we can say that a minute is "about" 50 seconds and an hour is "about" 50 minutes:

$$10,000 \text{ sec.} \approx 200 \text{ min.} \approx 4 \text{ hr.}$$

Similar estimates for other values of n and other big-O functions gives us the following table:

	1,000	5,000	10,000	50,000	100,000	500,000
				n		
$O(1)$	1 sec.	1 sec.	1 sec.	1 sec.	1 sec.	1 sec.
$O(\log n)$	1 sec.	1.2 sec.	1.3 sec.	1.6 sec.	1.7 sec.	1.9 sec.
$O(n)$	1 sec.	5 sec.	10 sec.	1 min.	2 min.	10 min.
$O(n^2)$	1 sec.	$\frac{1}{2}$ min.	2 min.	1 hr.	4 hr.	4 days
$O(2^n)$	1 sec.		more than $2 \times 10^{1,000}$ years			

If you graph these values, you can clearly see how the running time grows for each different big-O function as *n* gets larger: constant time gives a horizontal line; linear time a straight line that grows as *n* does; and quadratic time a parabola. Logarithmic and exponential times produce corresponding curves, the former growing very slowly, the latter incredibly quickly. These, of course, are not the only possibilities. Any function of *n* is a possible big-O description of an algorithm's efficiency. In particular, $O(n \log n)$ is a description that you will encounter fairly frequently.

2.4 FAST ENOUGH

From these estimates, you can see that, in general, logarithmic time is better than linear time, which is better than polynomial time, which is better than exponential time. Constant time is, of course, best of all. However, the "fastest" algorithm is not always the best choice.

What a big-O function actually describes is the *approximate growth rate* of the algorithm's running time. Because of the ignored terms and coefficients, a "slow" algorithm may actually run more quickly than a "fast" one for relatively small values of *n*. For example, the $O(\log n)$ binary search algorithm is more complex than the $O(n)$ linear search, so for small *n* the overhead of the extra instructions (not to mention the overhead of keeping the values of the array in order) may well overshadow its overall efficiency. Also, linear search is much easier to program correctly, saving programmer time. If you know that a collection is going to be fairly small, it may be better to use a linear search than the "more efficient" binary search.

Programming involves trade-offs, which can only be made with the knowledge of how each algorithm fits into the program as a whole; the algorithms do not exist in isolation. Sometimes, as in the earlier example, they involve using "fast enough" code that is easier to write rather than "efficient" code that is more likely to have bugs. Other times they are *time/space* trade-offs, which involve using a slower algorithm that uses less memory or using more memory to implement a faster algorithm. You will see examples of both in later chapters.

EXERCISE

In his 1953 short story "The Nine Billion Names of God," Arthur C. Clarke has a computer print each of the nine billion names. He estimates that it will take about 100 days. High-speed printers of that era could print about 150 lines per minute. Assuming that the computer could print 10 names per line, about how long would it actually have taken to print all nine billion names? How fast would the printer need to be to finish the job in 100 days? What do you think was the big-O complexity of the algorithm used? Why?

CHAPTER 3

LINKED LISTS

L   inked lists are unique among the classic data structures in that they
    are used primarily to implement other data structures. Everything
    you need to know about linked lists is contained in Figure 3.1.

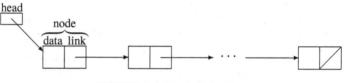

FIGURE 3.1 Singly-linked list

A *linked list* is a collection of *nodes*, each of which has a *data* field and a
link field. The data field holds an element of the list; the link field holds a
pointer to the node that holds the next data element (`nullptr` in the last
node). The first node in the list is called its *head*. The list is accessed via
a pointer to its head. Since there is one node for each data element, plus a
pointer, space requirements are $O(n)$. Unlike a vector, which may use up to
twice the space required for its elements, a linked list requires extra memory
only for $n + 1$ pointers. If the size of a data element is large compared to
the size of a pointer, a linked list is much more space-efficient than a vector,
even though both are $O(n)$ in that regard.

There are many variations on the basic, singly-linked list structure
shown in Figure 3.1. One possibility is a *doubly-linked* list, shown in Figure 3.2. Instead of a single link to the next node, each node has two links,
a *right link* to the next node and a *left link* to the previous one. Using a
doubly-linked list makes it easier to insert and delete nodes in the middle
of a list, at the expense of n extra pointers.

Another variant is the *circular-linked* list, where there is no natural

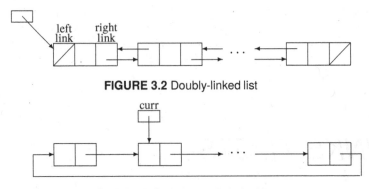

FIGURE 3.2 Doubly-linked list

FIGURE 3.3 Circular singly-linked list

head node. There is no null link at the end; the link field of each node points to another node, forming a circular chain. It therefore makes sense to call the list pointer in a circular list "curr" (for current) instead of "head." It is also possible to imagine a circular, doubly-linked list, as well as other variants.

Even though linked structures are straightforward, programming them can be tricky. The difficulty lies in keeping in mind the distinction between a pointer and the thing pointed at (as well as that between a node and a field in that node). This is why diagrams are so necessary. Whenever you have to implement a linked structure, work out your algorithm using a diagram (paying particular attention to these distinctions) before you put it into code. This will be difficult at first, so take it slowly. Eventually, it will become easier.

3.1 THE LIST INTERFACE

In addition to the usual member functions `size`, `empty`, `clear`, `begin`, and `end` (all of which are $O(1)$, except for `clear`, which is $O(n)$), the STL `list` class provides the following functions,

Accessors

front	$O(1)$	first element
back	$O(1)$	last element

Mutators

push_front	$O(1)$	add an element at the beginning
push_back	$O(1)$	add an element at the end
pop_front	$O(1)$	remove the first element
pop_back	$O(1)$	remove the last element
insert	$O(1)$	insert an element at a specified position
erase	$O(1)$	remove the element at a specified position

all of which run in constant time. It also provides a default constructor, which constructs an empty list in constant time, a $O(n)$ destructor, plus the usual assignment operator and copy/`initializer_list` constructors (which are all $O(n)$).

Unlike a vector, a linked list only allocates (and releases) space for elements as needed, so `capacity` and `resize` functions would be meaningless. Nor is it possible to index directly into a linked list, so `at` and the '`[]`' operator are equally meaningless. However, it is possible to add or remove any list element in constant time, which in a vector would involve relocating the elements that follow the added or removed element, a linear time operation. Hence the $O(1)$ functions `push_front`, `pop_front`, `insert`, and `erase`.

Since linked lists are used mostly for implementing other data structures, we'll use lists to implement stacks and queues in Chapter 4 instead of presenting a more artificial example here.

3.2 LIST IMPLEMENTATION

The layout of our `List` class is somewhat different than what you've already seen. This is because it requires "helper" classes and type aliases for its nodes and iterators.

⟨*interface for* `List` 43⟩≡
```
    template <typename T>
    class List {
    private:
        ⟨List helper classes 44b⟩
    public:
        ⟨List type aliases 51b⟩
        ⟨List constructor declarations 44c⟩
        ⟨List member function declarations 47a⟩
    private:
        ⟨List data members and private function declarations 44a⟩
    };
```
Helper classes are *nested* within the class declaration because they are needed only for `List` operations, and this keeps the names local. This way we can use the same name, "`Node`," for all such helpers in other classes. They are declared private to prevent any access outside the class. The public type aliases provide the limited outside access that is sometimes needed (by iterator classes, for example).

We represent a `List` as two pointers: one to the first node in the list and one to the last. We use `count` to keep track of the number of elements because the `size` function must run in constant time, and without it, `size` would have to traverse the entire list—a $O(n)$ operation—to count the nodes. A similar argument applies to the need for `last`, since `push_back` and `pop_back` must both be $O(1)$.

⟨List *data members and private function declarations* 44a⟩≡
```
    int count;        // number of nodes in list
    Node *first;      // pointer to first node
    Node *last;       // pointer to last node
```

We use a doubly-linked list, because node insertion or deletion requires ac-

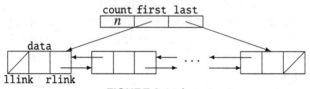

FIGURE 3.4 List structure

cess to the previous node as well as the specified one. Each `Node`, therefore, has two pointers—one to the next node (`rlink`), and one to the previous one (`llink`)—as well as a field to hold the data value. Figure 3.4 shows this structure.

The `Node` constructor, which assigns a value to the `data` field and `nullptr` to both link fields, is provided as a convenience, to save the trouble of extra assignment statements when allocating new nodes.

⟨List *helper classes* 44b⟩≡
```
  struct Node {
      T data;
      Node *rlink, *llink;           // forward (right) & back (left) links
      Node(const T& value = T())
          : data(value), rlink(nullptr), llink(nullptr) {}
  };
```

A C++ `struct` is merely a `class` where all members are public. `List` and iterator operations need access to a `Node`'s data members. Since `Node` is declared private, this allows them—but no others—the complete access they need.

3.2.1 Constructors/Destructors

The default constructor constructs an empty list, which has zero elements, no `first` node, and no `last` node, as shown in Figure 3.5.

⟨List *constructor declarations* 44c⟩≡
```
  List() : count(0), first(nullptr), last(nullptr) {}
```

count first last

| 0 | | |

FIGURE 3.5 Empty List

The destructor must release the space used by all of the nodes,

⟨List *constructor declarations* 44c⟩+≡

```
~List()
{
    ⟨delete all of a List's nodes 45b⟩
}
```

which involves following each `rlink` in turn, starting at the `first` node, and continuing until it reaches the final `nullptr`. The space for each node cannot be released until after its `rlink` has been traversed, hence the need for the temporary variable, `curr`.

⟨delete *all of a* List's *nodes* 45b⟩≡

```
while (first != nullptr) {
    Node *curr = first;
    first = first->rlink;
    delete curr;
}
```

The copy constructor is simple. After using the default constructor to create an empty `List`, it iterates through the `other` list, using `push_back` to add its elements to this one.

⟨List *constructor declarations* 44c⟩+≡

```
List(const List<T>& other) : List()
{
    for (auto p = other.begin(); p != other.end(); p++) {
        push_back(*p);
    }
}
```

The use of "`List()`" in the member initializer list to invoke the default constructor is called *constructor forwarding*, and is a C++11 construct, not available in earlier compilers. If your compiler does not support C++11, use "`count(0), first(0), last(0)`" instead of "`List()`" in the member initializer list (remember that `nullptr` is also a C++11 construct).

The `initializer_list` constructor works the same way as the copy constructor, except that it iterates through an `initializer_list` (`init`) rather than another `List`.

⟨List *constructor declarations* 44c⟩+≡

```
List(std::initializer_list<T> init) : List()
{
    for (auto p = init.begin(); p != init.end(); p++) {
        push_back(*p);
    }
}
```

To save time, our assignment operator copies data from the other list into corresponding existing nodes in this list, until it reaches the end of either list. If other has more elements than this, the extra elements are then appended to this. If not, the no-longer-needed nodes are removed. Note that only one of the chunks ⟨*append excess* src *elements to* this 46c⟩ or ⟨*remove no-longer-needed nodes* 46d⟩ will actually do anything.

⟨List *constructor declarations* 44c⟩+≡

```
List<T>& operator = (const List<T>& other)
{
    if (this != &other) {     // ignore assignment to self
        auto dest = begin();
        auto src = other.begin();
        ⟨copy src elements into existing dest elements 46b⟩
        ⟨append excess src elements to this 46c⟩
        ⟨remove no-longer-needed nodes 46d⟩
    }
    return *this;
}
```

We use standard iterator operations to copy values from one list to existing nodes in another.

⟨*copy* src *elements into existing* dest *elements* 46b⟩≡

```
for (; dest != end() and src != other.end(); src++,dest++) {
    *dest = *src;
}
```

When there are more elements in the source list than in the destination, we use push_back to add new nodes for the extras.

⟨*append excess* src *elements to* this 46c⟩≡

```
for (; src != other.end(); src++) { // size() < other.size()
    push_back(*src);
}
```

When there aren't enough elements in other to fill the nodes in this list, we use pop_back to remove the existing nodes that aren't needed anymore.

⟨*remove no-longer-needed nodes* 46d⟩≡

```
while (size() > other.size()) {      // size() > other.size()
    pop_back();
}
```

3.2.2 Member Functions

Accessors

Since the count data member keeps track of the number of elements, size simply reports its value, and empty depends on size.

⟨List *member function declarations* 47a⟩≡
```
int size() const { return count; }
bool empty() const { return size() == 0; }
```

The `front` element is contained in the `data` field of the node pointed to by `first`. As in `Vector`, we need both `const` and non-`const` versions.

⟨List *member function declarations* 47a⟩+≡
```
      T& front()       { return first->data; }
const T& front() const { return first->data; }
```

Similarly, the `back` element is contained in the `data` field of the node pointed to by `last`.

⟨List *member function declarations* 47a⟩+≡
```
      T& back()       { return last->data; }
const T& back() const { return last->data; }
```

Mutators

We use the `insert` and `erase` member functions to implement the push and pop operations, respectively. Both `front` operations use the `begin` iterator, but only `push_back` uses `end`. This is because the `end` iterator refers to a location *after* the last element, not to an actual element that can be removed. So we must construct an iterator that refers to the `last` node for `pop_back`.

⟨List *member function declarations* 47a⟩+≡
```
void push_front(const T& value) { insert(begin(), value); }
void push_back(const T& value)  { insert(end(), value); }
void pop_front() { erase(begin()); }
void pop_back()  { erase(iterator(last)); }
```

Inserting an element into a list requires pointer manipulation, so it's best to start with a diagram. Figure 3.6 shows the steps necessary to insert

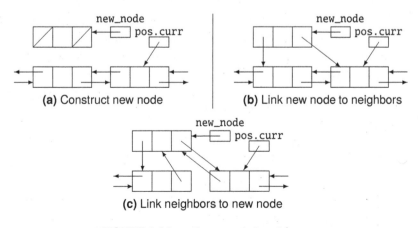

(a) Construct new node   **(b)** Link new node to neighbors

(c) Link neighbors to new node

FIGURE 3.6 Inserting a node in a `List`

a node into a doubly-linked list. The `pos` iterator passed to `insert` has a `curr` field that contains a pointer to the node before which the new node is to be inserted (see Section 3.2.3).

After constructing a new node (Figure 3.6a), the new node's right link is pointed to the `pos` node and its left link is pointed to the `pos` node's predecessor (Figure 3.6b). Then the `pos` node's `llink` and its predecessor's `rlink` are pointed at the new node (Figure 3.6c).

If the insertion is at the beginning or end of the list, it is necessary to adjust `first`, `last`, or both, to reflect the fact that the new node is now first or last in the chain. Finally, the new node is included in the element count and an iterator referring to the new node is returned.

⟨List *member function declarations* 47a⟩+≡
```
iterator insert(iterator pos, const T& value)
{
    Node *new_node = new Node(value);   //  Figure 3.6a
    ⟨link new_node to neighbor nodes 48b⟩     //  Figure 3.6b
    ⟨link neighbor nodes to new_node 48c⟩     //  Figure 3.6c
    ⟨adjust last and first, if necessary 49a⟩
    ++count;
    return iterator(new_node);
}
```

Linking a new node to its neighbors involves adjusting its link fields as shown in Figure 3.6b. A special case occurs when a node is being appended to the end of a list (when `pos.curr` equals `nullptr`). In this case, its `llink` is set to `last`, since `pos` has no node with an `llink` pointer to copy. Note that `rlink` gets set properly whether `pos.curr` is null or not.

⟨*link* new_node *to neighbor nodes* 48b⟩≡
```
new_node->rlink = pos.curr;
if (pos.curr == nullptr) { new_node->llink = last; }
else { new_node->llink = pos.curr->llink; }
```

Care must be taken when adjusting neighbor node links (Figure 3.6c), to deal with the possibility that there is no following node (the new node is last in the list) or there is no previous node (the new node is first in the list).

⟨*link neighbor nodes to* new_node 48c⟩≡
```
if (new_node->rlink != nullptr) {          // no following node
    new_node->rlink->llink = new_node;
}
if (new_node->llink != nullptr) {          // no previous node
    new_node->llink->rlink = new_node;
}
```

When inserting before begin(), new_node becomes the new first; when inserting before end(), it becomes the new last.

⟨*adjust* last *and* first, *if necessary* 49a⟩≡
```
if (pos == begin()) { first = new_node; }
if (pos == end())   { last = new_node; }
```

Removing a node from a list also involves pointer manipulation, as shown in Figure 3.7. The rlink of the previous node is pointed at the

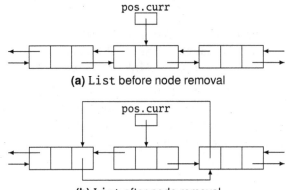

(a) List before node removal

(b) List after node removal

FIGURE 3.7 Removing a node from a List

following node, and the llink of the following node is pointed at the previous node.

At this point, the node is effectively removed from the list. Once the space for the node is released (using delete), it no longer matters what its link fields point to, and the element count is adjusted to reflect one less node in the list.

An iterator referring to the node that followed the removed one is returned. Since the space for the node it refers to has been released, the pos iterator is no longer valid.

⟨List *member function declarations* 47a⟩+≡
```
iterator erase(iterator pos)
{
    iterator result(pos.curr->rlink);
    ⟨link left neighbor's rlink to right neighbor 50a⟩
    ⟨link right neighbor's llink to left neighbor 50b⟩
    ⟨make sure end pointers are null 50c⟩
    delete pos.curr;
    --count;
    return result;
}
```

If we're removing the first node, we simply point `first` to the second node. If not, we point the previous node's `rlink` "around" the node we're removing to its successor.

⟨*link left neighbor's* `rlink` *to right neighbor* 50a⟩≡
```
if (pos.curr == first) { first = first->rlink; }
else { pos.curr->llink->rlink = pos.curr->rlink; }
```

If we're removing the last node, we simply point `last` to the next-to-last node. If not, we point the previous node's `llink` "around" the node we're removing to its predecessor.

⟨*link right neighbor's* `llink` *to left neighbor* 50b⟩≡
```
if (pos.curr == last) { last = last->llink; }
else { pos.curr->rlink->llink = pos.curr->llink; }
```

If the first or last node was removed (and there are still nodes in the list), it's possible that the `rlink` of the last node or the `llink` of the first node still points to the removed node. The following code chunk makes sure that both of these links are null (and does no harm if they already are).

⟨*make sure end pointers are null* 50c⟩≡
```
if (first != nullptr)
    { first->llink = last->rlink = nullptr; }
```

To clear a `List`, we release the space used by all of the nodes, and adjust the data members to indicate that it's empty (see Figure 3.5).

⟨`List` *member function declarations* 47a⟩+≡
```
void clear()
{
    ⟨delete all of a List's nodes 45b⟩
    first = last = nullptr;
    count = 0;
}
```

3.2.3 Iterators

We use another helper class to implement `List` iterators. Both `const` and non-`const` iterators are needed, but the code to implement them is almost exactly the same (the only difference being the keyword "`const`" in a few significant places), so we use a template class to implement `Iter`. We use U as the type placeholder instead of the more usual T because `Iter` is nested inside a template class that already uses T.

Our iterator is primarily a pointer to the current node in the iteration (`curr`). `List` operators such as `insert` and `erase` need access to the `curr` field, but we don't want it accessible to the world at large, so we declare it private and designate the `List<T>` class as a "friend," which specifies that `List` (and only `List`, in this case) operations can access `curr` and the constructor.

The iterator operators, on the other hand, must be available to all.

⟨List *helper classes* 44b⟩+≡
```
template <typename U>
class Iter {
private:
    Node *curr;
    friend class List<T>;
public:
    Iter(Node *p) : curr(p) {}
    ⟨List<T>::Iter operators 51c⟩
};
```

List<T>::iterator and List<T>::const_iterator are defined simply as Iter<T> and Iter<const T>, respectively. The aliases are, of course, public.

⟨List *type aliases* 51b⟩≡
```
typedef Iter<T> iterator;
typedef Iter<const T> const_iterator;
```

The * and -> operators provide access to the curr node's data field. Two List iterators are equal if and only if their curr fields point to the same node.

⟨List<T>::Iter *operators* 51c⟩≡
```
U& operator *  () const { return curr->data; }
U* operator -> () const { return &(curr->data); }
bool operator == (const Iter<U>& other) const
    { return curr == other.curr; }
bool operator != (const Iter<U>& other) const
    { return curr != other.curr; }
```

The ++ operators mimic the standard ++ operators. Incrementing an iterator moves curr along the node's rlink to point to the next node in the list. The prefix version increments the iterator and returns a reference to the incremented version; the postfix version returns a copy of the current iterator, which is then incremented.

⟨List<T>::Iter *operators* 51c⟩+≡
```
Iter<U>& operator ++ ()            // prefix ++
    { curr = curr->rlink; return *this; }
Iter<U> operator ++ (int)          // postfix ++
    { Iter<U> result = Iter<U>(curr); curr = curr->rlink;
        return result; }
```

An iteration starts with the first element, so our begin functions return an iterator that refers to the node pointed at by first.

⟨List *member function declarations* 47a⟩+≡
```
        iterator begin()       {return iterator(first);}
  const_iterator begin() const {return const_iterator(first);}
```

An iteration ends when its iterator passes the last node (i.e., when `curr` becomes null), so our **end** functions return an iterator that refers to `nullptr`.

⟨List *member function declarations* 47a⟩+≡
```
            iterator end()        {return iterator(nullptr);}
   const_iterator end() const {return const_iterator(nullptr);}
```

PROGRAMMING EXERCISE

For a doubly-linked list, as shown in Figure 3.4, the `insert` and `erase` functions have to deal with the special cases of insertion and deletion at the beginning or end of a list, because the first node has no predecessor and the last node has no successor. If the list were circular, with the last node's `rlink` pointing to the first node, and the first node's `llink` pointing to the last node, this would not be a problem. On the other hand, such a circular list makes it impossible to detect the end of an iteration. The solution is to use a "dummy" header node whose `rlink` points to the first node and `llink` points to the last node. Figure 3.8 shows such a list. The dummy

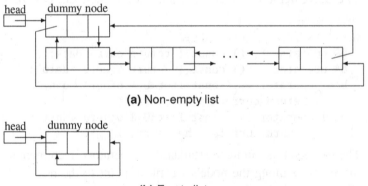

(a) Non-empty list

(b) Empty list

FIGURE 3.8 Circular, doubly-linked list with dummy header node

node serves as a marker for the end of an iteration, and removes the need for a separate pointer to the last node. The value in the `data` field of the dummy node is irrelevant.

Re-implement the `List` class using a circular, doubly-linked list with a dummy header node.

CHAPTER 4

STACKS AND QUEUES

S tacks and queues are data structures whose elements are ordered temporally, rather than spatially. The elements of a stack are organized in a *last-in-first-out* manner, the elements of a queue in a *first-in-first-out* manner. If you take a close look, you can see examples of each all around you. A group of people lining up* to buy tickets is a queue. The pile of papers on your desk is a stack. A stack of pancakes is, of course, a stack. And accountants have LIFO and FIFO techniques for managing inventory (stack and queue, respectively).

In computing, stacks are used for function calls, arithmetic, and parsing (among other things). Queues are used for task scheduling, process communication, and in simulations (again, among other things). The STL provides both `stack` and `queue` classes.

4.1 THE STACK AND QUEUE INTERFACES

The STL `stack` and `queue` classes do not provide iterators. Nor do they provide a `clear` function. But they do provide the usual `size` and `empty` operations.

The `stack` and `queue` interfaces are similar. They provide only limited access to the elements in the collection. Only the top of a stack is accessible. Elements are *pushed* onto a stack and *popped* off it.

---

*This is called "standing on line" in New York, "standing in line" in the rest of the United States, and "queueing up" in Britain. The last is most appropriate here.

Accessors (`stack`)

top	$O(1)$	top element

Mutators (`stack`)

push	$O(1)$	put an element on top
pop	$O(1)$	remove the top element

Only the front and rear of a queue are accessible. The `queue` interface uses the same terminology as `stack`: Elements are *pushed* into it at the rear and *popped* from the front.

Accessors (`queue`)

front	$O(1)$	element at the front
back	$O(1)$	element at the rear

Mutators (`queue`)

push	$O(1)$	append an element to the rear
pop	$O(1)$	remove the front element

All stack and queue operations run in constant time.

4.2 EXAMPLE: INFIX AND POSTFIX

An interesting example, using both stacks and queues, is *infix-to-postfix conversion*. *Infix* notation is the traditional way we write arithmetic expressions, with each operator between two operands. For example,

$$5 + 4 \times (9 - 3) \div 2 \tag{4.1}$$

The problem with infix notation is that, in order to get the correct answer of 17, you have to know that multiplication and division have higher precedence than addition and subtraction, and that parentheses can subvert precedence. A more logical notation is *postfix*, where an expression is read strictly from left to right, and each operator works with the two results immediately preceding it. In postfix notation, the expression (4.1) becomes

$$5 \; 4 \; 9 \; 3 \; - \; \times 2 \div + \tag{4.2}$$

which may seem a bit strange to you, but is much easier for a computer to process. In fact, many computer systems are designed with postfix expressions in mind. Expression 4.3 adds the redundant parentheses to 4.2, which may make things a bit clearer.

$$(5 \; ((\; 4 \; (9 \; 3 \; -) \times) \; 2 \div) \; +) \tag{4.3}$$

Translating an infix expression (preferred by humans) into its postfix equivalent (preferred by machines) is reasonably straightforward. This algorithm uses a stack to store lower precedence operators until it is time to add them to the postfix version; each expression is represented as a queue of "tokens."

Algorithm: Infix to Postfix Conversion

Input: *infix*, the infix expression, a queue of tokens
Ouput: *postfix*, the postfix expression, a queue of tokens
Require: *opstack*, a stack of operator tokens

> **while** *infix* isn't empty **do**
> > *token* ← next element from *infix*
> > **if** *token* is a left parenthesis **then**
> > > push *token* on *opstack*
> >
> > **else if** *token* is a right parenthesis **then**
> > > **while** top element of *opstack* ≠ left parenthesis **do**
> > > > append top element of *opstack* to *postfix*
> > >
> > > remove left parenthesis from *opstack*
> >
> > **else if** *token* is an operator **then**
> > > **while** *opstack* isn't empty
> > > > **and** priority(*token*) ≤ priority(*opstack*'s top)* **do**
> > > > > append top element of *opstack* to *postfix*
> > >
> > > push *token* on *opstack*
> >
> > **else**   // *token* is an operand
> > > append *token* to *postfix*
> >
> > **while** *opstack* isn't empty **do**
> > > append top element of *opstack* to *postfix*

Stacks can be used for evaluating postfix expressions. The postfix expression (4.2) could be evaluated as follows:

> **push** 5 on the stack
> **push** 4 on the stack
> **push** 9 on the stack
> **push** 3 on the stack
> **pop** top two values; **subtract**; **push** result on the stack
> **pop** top two values; **multiply**; **push** result on the stack
> **push** 2 on the stack
> **pop** top two values; **divide**; **push** result on the stack
> **pop** top two values; **add**; push result on the stack

The result (17 in this case) is what remains on top of the stack.

4.3 STACK **AND** QUEUE **IMPLEMENTATION**

Both our `Stack` and `Queue` classes can be implemented using the STL `list` class. Since the implementations are similar, let us develop them side-by-side. The only data member for each is a `list`, named `data`.

---

*Note: priority(left parenthesis) = 0.

Stack	**Queue**
⟨Stack *data members* 56a⟩≡	⟨Queue *data members* 56b⟩≡
std::list<T> data;	std::list<T> data;

4.3.1 Constructors/Destructors

When no constructors are declared for a class, the C++ compiler generates a default constructor, copy constructor, assignment operator, and destructor. Since we have no pointer members, the generated defaults do just fine.

4.3.2 Member Functions

Accessors

The `size` and `empty` functions simply "pass the buck" to the same-named `list` functions.

Stack	**Queue**
⟨Stack *functions* 56c⟩≡	⟨Queue *functions* 56d⟩≡
int size() const	int size() const
{ return data.size(); }	{ return data.size(); }
bool empty() const	bool empty() const
{ return data.empty(); }	{ return data.empty(); }

It's fairly obvious that we should use the `front` and `back` of the `list` as the `front` and `back` of a `Queue`, but which end of the list should we use for the `top` of a `Stack`? We could go either way here, but `back` is traditional. Plus, if we use `back`, we can change `data` to be a `vector`,

⟨Stack *data members* **⟦alternate⟧** 56e⟩≡
  std::vector<T> data;

instead of a `list`, and everything else in the implementation remains the same.

Stack	**Queue**
⟨Stack *functions* 56c⟩+≡	⟨Queue *functions* 56d⟩+≡
T& top()	T& front()
{ return data.back(); }	{ return data.front(); }
	T& back()
	{ return data.back(); }

Mutators

`Stack` elements are pushed on the top, and `Queue` elements at the rear, both of which are represented by the `back` of `data`.

Stack	**Queue**

⟨Stack *functions* 56c⟩+≡
```
void push(const T& value)
   { data.push_back(value); }
```

⟨Queue *functions* 56d⟩+≡
```
void push(const T& value)
   { data.push_back(value); }
```

Stack elements are popped from the top (back) and Queue elements from the front.

Stack	**Queue**

⟨Stack *functions* 56c⟩+≡
```
void pop()
   { data.pop_back(); }
```

⟨Queue *functions* 56d⟩+≡
```
void pop()
   { data.pop_front(); }
```

PROGRAMMING EXERCISE

Implement the infix to postfix algorithm in a function,

```
void infix_to_postfix(queue<string>& expr);
```

which takes a queue of string tokens (expr), representing a valid infix expression, and replaces it with the equivalent postfix expression. The obvious way to do this is with a local variable:

```
queue<string> postfix;
     ⋮   // infix-to-postfix conversion code
expr = postfix;
```

Receive extra credit if you can write your function without having to define a local queue variable to hold the postfix expression.

CHAPTER 5

RECURSION

*R*ecursion is a word that strikes fear into the hearts of novice programmers. But it shouldn't. Recursion is merely the logical extension
of top-down design and stepwise refinement. For example, look at
the problem of linear search through a linked list to find a value x. The
array-based algorithm in Section 2.1.1 can, of course, be modified slightly
to return a pointer to the node containing the value if it's there, the null
pointer if not:

> *curr* ← *head*
> **while** *curr* is not null **do**
>   **if** the data in the *curr* node = x **then**
>   **return** *curr*
>   *curr* ← *curr→link*
> **return** the null pointer

Alternately, you could use a top-down/stepwise approach on the problem, and find there are three possibilities, two of which are trivial,

1. The list is empty (*head* is null), in which case the value is obviously
   not there and the null pointer should be returned;

2. The value x is in the *head* node, in which case *head* should be
   returned; or

3. The remaining nodes need to be checked.

This translates directly into the following algorithm:

> **if** *head* is null **then**
>   **return** the null pointer
> **else if** the data in the *head* node = *x* **then**
>   **return** *head*
> **else**
>   ⟨check if *x* can be found from *head→link*; return result⟩

Note that the non-trivial case is in English, to be refined later. Alternatively, it could have been replaced with a call to a to-be-defined-later function, such as

> **return** *check_rest_of_list*(*head→link, x*)

Either technique will produce an equivalent result.

The next step is to define an algorithm for ⟨check if *x* can be found from *head→link*; return result ⟩ or *check_rest_of_list*. There are, again, three possibilities:

1. *head→link* is null, in which case the value is obviously not there and the null pointer should be returned;

2. The value *x* is in the *head→link* node, in which case *head→link* should be returned; or

3. The remaining nodes need to be checked.

This looks suspiciously like the earlier three possibilities, and leads to the following algorithm,

> ⟨check if *x* can be found from *head→link*; return result⟩≡
>   **if** *head→link* is null **then**
>   **return** the null pointer
>   **else if** the data in the *head→link* node = *x* **then**
>   **return** *head→link*
>   **else**
>   ⟨check if *x* can be found from *head→link→link*; return result⟩

which is exactly the same as the previous algorithm, except that it replaces every "*head*" in the original version with "*head→link*." But using names as placeholders for values is exactly what parameters are for. So the solution is to designate the algorithm a function (*search*) with two parameters (*head* and *x*), and realize that the function must work on any list represented as a pointer to a node, even if that pointer is in a link field. That, in fact, the link field in a linked list node is itself a linked list.

Algorithm: *search*(*head, x*)

> **if** *head* is null **then**
>> **return** the null pointer
>
> **else if** the data in the *head* node = *x* **then**
>> **return** *head*
>
> **else**
>> **return** *search*(*head→link, x*)

This algorithm can be translated directly into a C++ function, assuming the types Node and T are defined appropriately.

```
Node *search(Node *head, const T& x)
{
    if (head == nullptr) { return nullptr; }
    else if (head->data == x) { return head; }
    else { return search(head->link, x); }
}
```

With slight modifications, the *search* algorithm can be generalized to search any container, specifying the iterators *start* and *stop* to mark the beginning and end of the search, instead of using *head* (and the implied null pointer) as in the linked list search,

Algorithm: *search*(*start, stop, x*)

> **if** *start* is the same as *stop* **then**
>> **return** *stop*   // not there
>
> **else if** the data at *start* = *x* **then**
>> **return** *start*
>
> **else**
>> **return** *search*(++*start, stop, x*)

which similarly translates directly into an equivalent C++ function template.

```
template <typename Iter, typename T>
Iter search(Iter start, Iter stop, const T& x)
{
    if (start == stop) { return stop; }
    else if (*start == x) { return start; }
    else { return search(++start, stop, x); }
}
```

In fact, recursion and iteration are functionally identical. Every loop can be converted into an equivalent recursive algorithm, and every recursive algorithm can be converted into an equivalent loop-based algorithm (which may need a stack).

5.1 RECURSIVE DEFINITIONS

A *recursive definition* is one that is partially in terms of the thing being defined. Until now, we have deliberately avoided the recursive definition of a list,

A list is either empty or a data element followed by a list,

although we did skate around it a bit.

A recursive definition consists of one or more *base cases*, and one or more *recursive cases*. In the definition of a list, the base case is an empty list, and the recursive case is a single element followed by a list.

You have probably already encountered the recursive definition of the set of natural numbers (sometimes referred to as the "positive integers"), $\mathbb{N} = \{1, 2, 3, \ldots\}$,

1 is a natural number;
If n is a natural number, then $n + 1$ is a natural number;

or, expressed symbolically,

$1 \in \mathbb{N}$;
$\forall n \in \mathbb{N}, n + 1 \in \mathbb{N}$.

Things defined recursively, such as lists, lend themselves to recursive functions. For example, the factorial function, $n!$, can be defined recursively for all non-negative integers,

$$n! = \begin{cases} 1 & \text{if } n = 0 \\ n \times (n - 1)! & \text{otherwise} \end{cases}$$

which translates directly into an equivalent C++ function (ignoring the possibility of negative n),

```
int fact(int n)
{
    if (n == 0) { return 1; }
    else { return n * fact(n - 1); }
}
```

A direct translation of a recursive definition into a recursive C++ function can be shown to be correct simply by comparing the code to the definition, and ensuring that they are equivalent.

5.2 PROOF BY INDUCTION

The proof technique called *mathematical induction* is based on the recursive definition of the natural numbers, and is used to prove that a given formula holds true for all of the natural numbers. The first step is to prove that the formula holds true for 1 (the *base case*). This is usually trivial. The next step is to assume that the formula holds true for some value k (the *induction hypothesis*), and show that if this is true, then the formula must hold true for the value $k + 1$. These two steps are sufficient to show that the formula must hold true for every value $1, 1 + 1 = 2, 2 + 1 = 3, 3 + 1 = 4, \ldots$ (in other words, every possible positive integer).

For example, the "well-known formula" used in analyzing the run-time efficiency of a bubble sort (Section 2.1.1),

$$\sum_{i=1}^{n} i = 1 + 2 + \cdots + n = \frac{n \times (n + 1)}{2},$$

which crops up fairly frequently in the analysis of $O(n^2)$ algorithms, can easily be proven by induction.

Prove the base case ($\sum_{i=1}^{1} i = \frac{1 \times (1+1)}{2}$): This is, of course, trivial.

$$\sum_{i=1}^{1} i = 1 = \frac{2}{2} = \frac{1 \times 2}{2} = \frac{1 \times (1 + 1)}{2}.$$

Assume $\sum_{i=1}^{k} i = \frac{k \times (k+1)}{2}$, **prove** $\sum_{i=1}^{k+1} i = \frac{(k+1) \times ((k+1)+1)}{2}$: A little bit of algebra proves this, given that $\sum_{i=1}^{k+1} i$ must equal $\left(\sum_{i=1}^{k} i \right)$ plus $(k + 1)$.

$$\sum_{i=1}^{k+1} i = \left(\sum_{i=1}^{k} i \right) + (k + 1) = \frac{k \times (k + 1)}{2} + (k + 1)$$
$$= \frac{k \times (k + 1)}{2} + \frac{2k + 2}{2}$$
$$= \frac{k \times (k + 1) + 2k + 2}{2} = \frac{k^2 + 3k + 2}{2}$$
$$= \frac{(k + 1) \times (k + 2)}{2}$$
$$= \frac{(k + 1) \times ((k + 1) + 1)}{2}.$$

As you may have suspected, given that both recursive definitions and proofs by inductions have a "base case," induction can be used to prove the correctness of recursive algorithms, notably those involving collections.

First you prove that the algorithm produces the correct result for the base case (usually $n = 0$, an empty collection). Then you assume that the algorithm works for a collection of k elements, and prove that it must work for $k + 1$ elements. To prove that the algorithm eventually halts, you have to show that each recursive call works on a smaller collection.

For the recursive *search* algorithm described earlier, the base cases are correct: (1) an empty list has no elements, and obviously, cannot contain x, and (2) if the first list element contains x, it is equally obvious that list contains x in the first position. The algorithm correctly returns the null pointer or *head*, respectively, for these cases.

Assuming that *search* works for a list of k elements, it's fairly simple to show that it must work for a list of $k + 1$ elements. The null case is irrelevant here, since an empty list cannot have $k + 1$ elements, regardless of the value of k. If the value of x is in the first node, the algorithm will correctly return *head*, and the recursive case operates on a list of $(k + 1) - 1 = k$ elements, which must produce the correct result according to the induction hypothesis. Each recursive call operates on a smaller (by one) list, so the algorithm must terminate. Therefore *search* is correct.

Proving the correctness of the iterative version is much more difficult.

5.3 EXAMPLE: BINARY SEARCH

The binary search algorithm (Section 2.1.1) can easily be expressed recursively,

> **Algorithm:** *binary_search(a, x, lower, upper)*
> _____
> **if** *lower* > *upper* **then**
>   **return** -1
> **else**
>   *mid* ← *(lower + upper)* ÷ 2
>   **if** *a[mid]* = *x* **then**
>   **return** *mid*
>   **else if** *a[mid]* < *x* **then**
>   **return** *binary_search(a, x, mid + 1, upper)*
>   **else**   // *a[mid]* > *x*
>   **return** *binary_search(a, x, lower, mid − 1)*

and the recursive version can easily be proved correct by induction. The base case when the number of elements, n, is zero, is trivially true. The next step is to assume that the search works for every array from zero up to k elements,[*] and to prove that it must also work for $k + 1$ elements.

In a $(k + 1)$-element array, if the value x is in the middle element, the algorithm correctly returns the index of the middle element. Otherwise,

_____

[*]This is known as the *strong form* of the induction hypothesis, and although it seems more powerful, is actually equivalent to the "weak" form.

binary_search is called recursively on the range $a[mid+1]$ through $a[upper]$ when the value of x is less than that at the midpoint, and on the range $a[lower]$ through $a[mid-1]$ otherwise. In either case, the length of the new range to search is less than or equal to $\frac{k+1}{2}$. Since $\frac{k+1}{2}$ is less than or equal to k for all positive integers, the induction hypothesis is enough to prove that the recursive cases are correct. The same fact demonstrates that each recursive call works on a smaller piece of the array, so the algorithm is guaranteed to halt.

It's also fairly easy to see that, on average, the algorithm runs in logarithmic time. Each recursive call operates on an interval at most one half the size of the current one, and there is, at most, one recursive call for each interval, so there can be, at most, $\lceil \log_2 n \rceil$ calls to *binary_search*, each of which runs in constant time. Therefore, the algorithm is $O(\log n)$.

5.4 EXAMPLE: TOWER OF HANOI

The puzzle known as the Tower of Hanoi (often referred to in the plural) was introduced by the French mathematician Édouard Lucas in 1883, along with a legend about its origins. The legend appears in many variations, and is irrelevant here, but is worth looking up if you have the time. The tower (Figure 5.1) consists of a number of discs of different sizes, and three

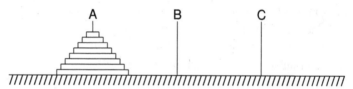

FIGURE 5.1 Tower of Hanoi

spindles on which the discs are stacked. Initially, the discs are all stacked on spindle A in order of size, with the largest disc on the bottom. The object of the puzzle is to move the tower, one disc at a time, to spindle C, with the restriction that no disc may be placed on top of a smaller one. Spindle B can be used as an auxiliary, a "resting place" for discs in transit.

The solution to this puzzle provides an excellent example of recursive thinking. If there are n discs on the spindle A, and you can figure out how to move $n-1$ discs to spindle B using C as the auxiliary (Figure 5.2), then

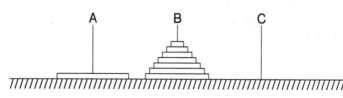

FIGURE 5.2 Tower of Hanoi: First stage of algorithm ·

all you have to do is move the remaining (largest) disc to spindle C, and move the discs on spindle B to spindle C the same way you moved them from A to B, but using A as the auxiliary this time. This reasoning leads to the recursive *hanoi* algorithm, which moves *n* discs from the *src* spindle to the *dest* spindle.

> **Algorithm:** *hanoi(n, src, dest, aux)*
> _____
> **if** *n* > 0 **then**
>   *hanoi(n − 1, src, aux, dest)*
>   move 1 disc from *src* to *dest*
>   *hanoi(n − 1, aux, dest, src)*

The proof by induction of *hanoi*'s correctness is equally simple. The base case ($n = 0$) is trivially correct, as the algorithm does nothing when there are no discs on *src*. Assuming that *hanoi* correctly moves a stack of *k* discs from *src* to *dest*, if it is used to move a stack of $k + 1$ discs, then the induction hypothesis ensures that the first recursive call successfully moves $(k + 1) − 1 = k$ discs from *src* to *aux*, and the second moves the same *k* discs from *aux* to *dest*. The remaining spindle in each instance must either be empty or contain a disc larger than all those being moved, so it can be safely used as auxiliary. The step that moves a single disc from *src* to *dest* is, of course, trivially correct. Therefore, the algorithm is correct.

As for efficiency, each non-zero call invokes *hanoi* twice. This doubling goes on to a depth of *n* calls, which means that the number of calls approaches 2^n, which means the algorithm is $O(2^n)$. In fact, the number of moves required to move an *n*-disc tower will always be $2^n − 1$, so any algorithm that solves the puzzle must be $O(2^n)$.

5.5 EXAMPLE: RECURSIVE DESCENT PARSING

Perhaps the most interesting (and useful) application of recursion is *recursive descent parsing*. This is best illustrated with an example. An infix expression can be defined recursively:

> An *expression* is a sequence of one or more *terms* separated by additive operators ('+' or '−'),

> A *term* is a sequence of one or more *factors* separated by multiplicative operators ('*' or '/'),

> A *factor* is either an integer constant, or an *expression* enclosed in parentheses.

These definitions can also be expressed expressed graphically:

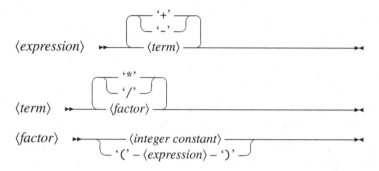

Unlike the other definitions in this chapter, these are *indirectly* recursive: no definition invokes itself directly, but each can cause a chain of invocations that will eventually recurse (because "expression" is defined using "term," which is defined using "factor," which is defined using "expression").

These definitions use recursion to embody the usual precedence rules, with "deeper" levels having higher precedence, and can be translated directly into algorithms, one for each rule,

> **Algorithm:** *parse_expr*
>
> *parse_term*
> **while** *next_token* = '+' or '-' **do**
> *parse_term*

> **Algorithm:** *parse_term*
>
> *parse_factor*
> **while** *next_token* = '*' or '/' **do**
> *parse_factor*

> **Algorithm:** *parse_factor*
>
> **if** *next_token* ≠ '(' **then**
> *next_token* must be an integer constant
> **else**
> *next_token* must be a '('
> *parse_expr*
> *next_token* must be a ')'

which, taken together, recognize any valid infix expression much more elegantly than the infix-to-postfix algorithm in Section 4.2.

5.6   THE EFFICIENCY OF RECURSION

In general, recursive functions have the same big-O efficiency as their iterative counterparts. Recursion is usually implemented using a stack, which means that extra memory is required for each recursive call, in addition to the overhead for the function call, so that recursive functions are often derided as "inefficient." However, a simple recursive function based on a recursive algorithm that can be proved correct will save a great deal of programmer time in exchange for the extra memory requirements, and programmer time is much more expensive than both memory and computer time. Unless the recursion is excessive, a recursive function can often be the best choice.

In addition, many recursive functions are what is called *tail-recursive*, meaning that the very last thing the function does before returning is to invoke itself. It is possible to automatically convert a tail-recursive function into an iterative one, eliminating both the function call and stack memory overhead. Many C++ compilers, including both the GNU and Visual Studio compilers, provide this capability as an option.

Except for recursive descent parsing, all the examples in this chapter are strictly tail-recursive. Only the second recursive call in the *hanoi* algorithm can be automatically converted to iteration, however. The first must remain recursive.

PROGRAMMING EXERCISE

Rewrite the

```
void infix_to_postfix(queue<string>& expr);
```

function from Chapter 4 using recursive descent in place of the earlier algorithm. Extra credit (again) for doing this without using a local **queue** variable to hold the resulting postfix expression.

BINARY TREES

D efined recursively, a *binary tree* is either 1) empty, or 2) a node with exactly two *children*, each of which is a binary tree.

Figure 6.1 gives some examples of binary trees. The initial node is called the *root*.* A node whose children are both empty is called a *leaf*.

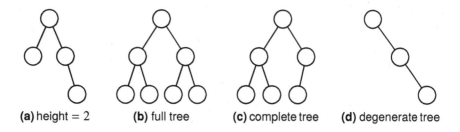

(a) height = 2   **(b)** full tree   **(c)** complete tree   **(d)** degenerate tree

FIGURE 6.1 Examples of binary trees

The *height* of a binary tree is the length of the longest path from the root to a leaf. A *full tree* (Figure 6.1b) is one where every node is either a leaf or has two non-empty children. A full tree or one that would be full except that it is missing the rightmost nodes in the lowest level is called a *complete tree* (Figure 6.1c). A tree in which each non-leaf node has only one non-empty child is called *degenerate* (Figure 6.1d).

Traditional relationship terminology is often applied to nodes in a tree. A *child* node is obviously the root node of one of a non-leaf node's child

---

*The root is at the top of the tree rather than the bottom because it's easier to draw that way.

trees. The meaning of the terms *parent, ancestor, descendant,* and *sibling* all follow naturally from this.

6.1 TRAVERSALS

There are three different ways to traverse a binary tree, *visiting* each node to perform some operation or other (such as printing the node's value): *preorder, postorder,* and *inorder* traversals. The prefixes *pre-, post-,* and *in-* specify the point in the traversal where the "visit" occurs. Each can be described by a recursive algorithm.

A preorder traversal visits the root node first, and then traverses the left child and right child trees, in that order.

Algorithm: *traverse_preorder(root)*

if *root* is not null **then**
　　visit the current node
　　traverse_preorder(root→lchild)
　　traverse_preorder(root→rchild)

For example, a preorder traversal of the following tree

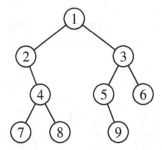

would visit nodes in the order 1 2 4 7 8 3 5 9 6.

A postorder traversal visits the root last, after traversing the left and right child trees, respectively,

Algorithm: *traverse_postorder(root)*

if *root* is not null **then**
　　traverse_postorder(root→lchild)
　　traverse_postorder(root→rchild)
　　visit the current node

and would visit the nodes of the above tree in the order 7 8 4 2 9 5 6 3 1.

An inorder traversal visits the root node after traversing the left child tree, but before visiting the right child tree,

Algorithm: *traverse_inorder(root)*

if *root* is not null **then**
　　traverse_inorder(root→lchild)
　　visit the current node
　　traverse_inorder(root→rchild)

and would visit the nodes of the above tree in the order 2 7 4 8 1 5 9 3 6.

Each of these traversal types is useful in its own way, as you will see. Since they visit each node of a tree exactly once, all three traversal algorithms are $O(n)$.

6.2 EXAMPLE: EXPRESSION TREES

Expressions involving binary operations can be represented by binary trees. For example, the infix expression $5 \times (4 + 27 \div 3) + 7$ could be represented by the binary tree,

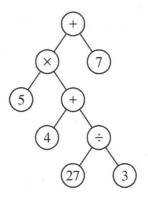

which specifies unambiguously the order in which the operations should be performed, with the lower nodes representing operations performed early in the evaluation and the root node operation performed last.

Since there are two kinds of nodes—operations and values—expression tree node types are prime candidates for inheritance, with value and operation node classes derived from an abstract expression node base class (see the programming exercise at the end of the chapter). Each class might provide an *eval* member function that evaluates its expression using a postorder traversal of the tree,

> **Algorithm:** *eval()*   // for a value node
>   **return** *this→data*
> **Algorithm:** *eval()*   // for an operation node
>   **return** *this→lchild→eval()* **op** *this→rchild→eval()*

where **op** is the specific operation (+ − ×÷) represented by each operation node type. Note that even though the operation, **op**, appears between the two child tree evaluations, it is not performed until *after* both children have been evaluated.

Similarly, an inorder traversal can be used to print out an expression tree in infix form with the minimum number of parentheses.

Algorithm: *print_infix()*   // for a value node

print *this→data*

Algorithm: *print_infix()*   // for an operation node

  if *this→priority* < *this→parent→priority* **then**

    print '('

this→lchild→print_infix()

print the appropriate operation symbol

this→rchild→print_infix()

  if *this→priority* < *this→parent→priority* **then**

    print ')'

6.3 EXAMPLE: BINARY SEARCH TREES

A *binary search tree* is a binary tree in which every node has the property that every value in its left child tree is less than the node's value, and every value in its right child tree is greater than the node's value. Figure 6.2 is an

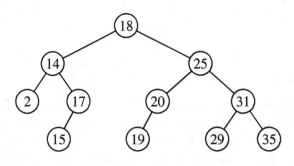

FIGURE 6.2 Binary search tree

example of a binary search tree.

Inorder traversal of a binary search tree visits its nodes in order of their values, from lowest to highest. An inorder traversal of Figure 6.2, therefore, visits its nodes in the order 2 14 15 17 18 19 20 25 29 31 35.

Finding a value in a binary search tree involves a kind of cross between a recursive linked list search and a binary search. If the tree is empty, return a null pointer, indicating that the value is not there. If the value is in the root node, return a pointer to that node. Otherwise, check to see if the value is less or greater than the root node value, and search the left or right subtree, respectively.

Algorithm: *search*(*root*, *x*)
___
    if *root* is null **then**
        return the null pointer
    else if $x = root{\to}data$ **then**
        return *root*
    else if $x < root{\to}data$ **then**
        return *search*(*root*{\to}*lchild*, *x*)
    else   // $x > root{\to}data$
        return *search*(*root*{\to}*rchild*, *x*)

Adding a new value involves traversing the tree (as in *search*) to find where to add the new node. Duplicate insertions are ignored. Using a reference parameter for the root simplifies the algorithm by allowing a single assignment to change either the original root or one of the child pointers, depending on what's been passed as a parameter.

Algorithm: *add*(*root*, *x*)
___
Require: *root* is a reference parameter
    if *root* is null **then**
        root ← a new node containing *x*
    else if $x = root{\to}data$ **then**
        do nothing—ignore duplicate insertions
    else if $x < root{\to}data$ **then**
        add(*root*{\to}*lchild*, *x*)
    else   // $x > root{\to}data$
        add(*root*{\to}*rchild*, *x*)

Removing a value also requires a traversal to find the node to remove. This algorithm quietly ignores attempts to remove a value that isn't in the tree. Removing a single node once it has been located is somewhat tricky, so that problem is handled by a separate *remove_node* algorithm. As with *add*, using reference parameters somewhat simplifies things.

Algorithm: *remove*(*root*, *x*)
___
Require: *root* is a reference parameter
    if *root* is null **then**
        do nothing—*x* is not in tree
    else if $x = root{\to}data$ **then**
        remove_node(*root*)
    else if $x < root{\to}data$ **then**
        remove(*root*{\to}*lchild*, *x*)
    else   // $x > root{\to}data$
        remove(*root*{\to}*rchild*, *x*)

There are three possibilities for *remove_node*:

1. The node to be removed is a leaf, in which case it can simply be detached from the tree (Figure 6.3);

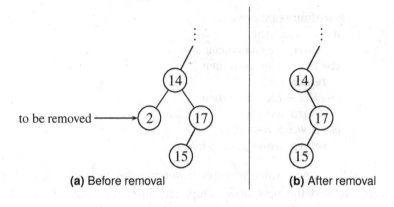

FIGURE 6.3 Removing a leaf from a binary search tree

2. The node to be removed has only one child, in which case the node can be replaced by the child (Figure 6.4); or

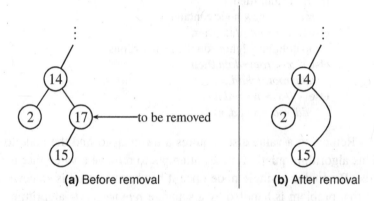

FIGURE 6.4 Removing a single-child node from a binary search tree

3. The node to be removed has two children, in which case the following steps are necessary:

   (a) Find the node's *inorder successor*—the node that would follow this one in an inorder traversal,

   (b) Replace the node's data with its inorder successor's data, and

   (c) Remove the inorder successor node. Since the inorder successor cannot have a left child (think about it), only case 1 or case 2 can apply here.

These translate directly into the following algorithm:

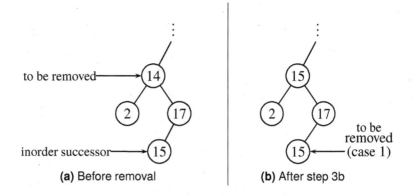

FIGURE 6.5 Removing a two-child node from a binary search tree

Algorithm: *remove_node(curr)*

Require: *curr* is a reference parameter

    if *curr→lchild* and *curr→rchild* are both null **then**
        free space pointed to by *curr*
        curr ← the null pointer
    else if only one child (call it "*child*") is non-null **then**
        tmp ← *curr*
        curr ← *child*
        free space pointed to by *tmp*
    else   // both child pointers are non-null
        successor ← *inorder_successor(curr)*
        curr→data ← *successor→data*
        remove_node(successor)

Finding the inorder successor of a node is relatively straightforward.

Algorithm: *inorder_successor(curr)*

Require: *curr* is not null

    if *curr→rchild* is not null **then**
        ⟨slide *curr* down left from its right child⟩
    else
        ⟨set *curr* to its first non-right-child ancestor⟩
    return *curr*

If the node has a right child (as must be the case when this algorithm is invoked by *remove_node*), starting at that child and "sliding down" left child pointers does the trick.

    ⟨slide *curr* down left from its right child⟩≡
        curr ← *curr→rchild*
        while *curr→lchild* is not null **do**
            curr ← *curr→lchild*

Otherwise, the inorder successor must be the parent node of a left child already traversed, so the ancestors of the current node must be traversed until one is found via a left child link.

> ⟨set *curr* to its first non-right-child ancestor⟩≡
>   *prev* ← *curr*
>   *curr* ← *curr→parent*
>   **while** *curr* is not null and *prev* = *curr→rchild* **do**
>   *prev* ← *curr*
>   *curr* ← *curr→parent*

If a tree is reasonably balanced, its height is close to $\log_2 n$ (where n is the number of nodes in the tree), so the longest traversal passes through about $\log_2 n$ nodes, making the *search*, *add*, and *remove* algorithms, on average, $O(\log n)$. If a tree is degenerate, however, the tree's height is exactly $n - 1$, and the traversal is $O(n)$.

The analysis of *inorder_successor* is fairly complex, and depends a great deal on how it is used. Suffice it to say that its run-time complexity amortizes to $O(1)$.

6.4 THE SET AND MAP INTERFACES

Binary search trees are represented in the STL by the `set` and `map` classes. The former provides the functionality of a mathematical set: a value is either contained in the set or not. The latter provides a "mapping" of one type of value (the *key*) onto another. The iterators for both classes provide inorder tree traversals.

In addition to the usual member functions `size`, `empty`, `clear`, `begin`, and `end` (all of which are $O(1)$, except for `clear`, which is $O(n)$), the `set` class provides the following functions,

Accessors

`count`	$O(\log n)$	the number of elements matching a given value

Mutators

`insert`	$O(\log n)$	insert a given value
`erase`	$O(\log n)$	remove a given value

Since duplicate entries are not allowed, the `count` function can only return one or zero, and can be used as a kind of "contains" function.

The `map` class is similar, but instead of containing simple values, it contains *key-value pairs*. Therefore, it provides the indexing operator ('`[]`') and `at` in place of `insert` (`at` was introduced in C++11).

Accessors

count	$O(\log n)$	number of elements matching a given key
[] operator	$O(\log n)$	reference to the value matching given key; default value inserted if no such key exists
at	$O(\log n)$	reference to value matching given key; exception if no such key exists

Mutators

erase	$O(\log n)$	remove the element with a given key

A key-value pair, **k** and **v**, can be inserted into a map, **m**, using the indexing operator:

```
m[k] = v;
```

If a pair with the key, **k**, already exists in the map, **v** replaces the existing value in the pair. If the '[]' operator is used on a map with a key that doesn't already exist, an element with that key and a default value is inserted into the map; if **at** is used in the same situation, an **out_of_range** exception is thrown (the '[]' operator is not strictly an accessor, and cannot be used with **const** maps; **at** must be used instead). As with **set**, **count** returns only one or zero.

The STL **pair** class (defined in the **<utility>** header) is used to maintain the key-value pairs. A **pair** has two public data members, **first** and **second**. The **make_pair** function provides a simple way to construct **pair** objects.

The **map** iterators provide access to the **pair** stored in the tree, with **first** containing the key and **second** its associated value.

6.5 EXAMPLE: ASSOCIATIVE ARRAYS

An *associative array* is essentially an array that can be indexed by a value other than an integer (usually a string type). For example, if **tally** maps strings onto integers (**map<string,int>**), the expression "tally["cat"]" might represent the number of times the string **"cat"** has been recognized by the program. If we define a "word" as any non-blank sequence of characters, the C++ code

```
string word;
while (cin >> word) {
    tally[word]++;
}
```

keeps count of the number of times each word appears in the standard input, and

```
for (auto p = tally.begin(); p != tally.end(); p++) {

    cout << p->first << ":  " << p->second << endl;
}
```

prints a list of all the words (in lexicographic order) along with their respective tallies.

6.6 EXAMPLE: SPARSE MATRICES

Very often in computing, it is necessary to deal with large amounts of data, most of which has some fixed, default value. If the data is conceptually a large two-dimensional array, this structure is called a *sparse matrix*. A C++ map provides an excellent way to implement a Sparse_Matrix class:

```
template <typename T>
class Sparse_Matrix {
        ⋮
private:
    map <pair<int,int>, T> data;
};
```

By defining a nested helper class that provides the '[]' operator to refer to a single row of the matrix,

```
struct Slice {
    Sparse_Matrix *mat;
    int row;
    Slice (Sparse_Matrix *m, int r)
        : mat(m), row(r) {}
    T& operator [] (int col)
        { return mat->data[make_pair(row, col)]; }
};
```

it's possible to use standard two-dimensional array notation, a[i][j], where a is a Sparse_Matrix, to access the matrix elements. All that's necessary is to define a '[]' operator that returns a Slice:

```
Slice Sparse_Matrix::operator [] (int row)
        { return Slice(this, row); }
```

6.7 A BINARY_SEARCH_TREE CLASS

Since binary search trees are used for implementing both the STL's set and map classes, it makes sense to define a Binary_Search_Tree class as a basis for our Set and Map class implementations.

The layout of `Binary_Search_Tree` is similar to that of `List` (Section 3.2). The only significant difference is the extra template parameter, `Compare`, which defaults to the standard class `less<T>`. The `less` class describes a *function object*: an object whose class implements the '`()`' operator so it can be used like a function. The '`()`' operator for `less` simply returns the result of the < operator on its two operands. The `<functional>` header, which defines `less`, also defines `greater`, `equal_to` and other useful function classes.

The `Compare` parameter allows you to use any function you want for ordering the tree; you can even define your own (as we will for the `Map` class; see Section 6.8). However, if nothing else is specified, `less<T>` is used.

⟨*interface for* `Binary_Search_Tree` 79a⟩≡

```
template <typename T, typename Compare = std::less<T> >
class Binary_Search_Tree {
private:
    ⟨Binary_Search_Tree helper classes 80a⟩
public:
    ⟨Binary_Search_Tree type aliases 88c⟩
    ⟨Binary_Search_Tree constructor declarations 80b⟩
    ⟨Binary_Search_Tree member function declarations 83a⟩
private:
    ⟨Binary_Search_Tree data members 79b⟩
    ⟨Binary_Search_Tree private function declarations 81a⟩
};
```

To represent a tree, we need a pointer to the root node, and a count of the number of nodes currently in the tree. The latter is necessary (as for `List`) so that the `size` function runs in constant time. We use the name `num_nodes` instead of `count` here because the latter must be the name of a member function.

⟨`Binary_Search_Tree` *data members* 79b⟩≡

```
Node *root;
int num_nodes;
```

To ensure that the `begin` function is $O(1)$, we use `first` to keep track of the initial iteration node. The `cmp` data member isn't really necessary, but it allows us to avoid the (slightly) awkward construct "`Compare()(a,b)`" by using the more natural "`cmp(a,b)`."

⟨`Binary_Search_Tree` *data members* 79b⟩+≡

```
Node *first;
Compare cmp;
```

A `Binary_Search_Tree` node (Figure 6.6) is similar to that for a doubly-linked list, with two child pointers. The only significant difference is a pointer to the parent node, which is necessary for implementing iterators.

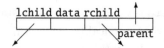

FIGURE 6.6 `Binary_Search_Tree` Node structure

As with `List`'s node class, a constructor is provided primarily as a convenience. The parent pointer is specified as the first parameter because it is the most likely to need a non-null value when a node is constructed.

⟨Binary_Search_Tree *helper classes* 80a⟩≡
```
struct Node {
    T data;
    Node *lchild, *rchild;
    Node *parent;
    Node(const T& item, Node *p = nullptr,
            Node *left = nullptr, Node *right = nullptr)
        : data(item), lchild(left), rchild(right),
          parent(p) {}
};
```

6.7.1 Constructors/Destructors

The default constructor constructs an empty tree. It's not necessary to initialize `cmp` because all we care about is its '`()`' operator, which doesn't access `this`. This constructor (obviously) runs in constant time.

⟨Binary_Search_Tree *constructor declarations* 80b⟩≡
```
Binary_Search_Tree()
    : root(nullptr), num_nodes(0), first(nullptr) {}
```

Like most of the `Binary_Search_Tree` member functions, the destructor requires a tree traversal, which in turn, requires recursion. It is often simpler to call a recursive helper function rather than making the member function itself recursive, so that's what we do. In any event, a destructor cannot be recursive, so we have to use a helper function, `free_all_nodes` here.

⟨Binary_Search_Tree *constructor declarations* 80b⟩+≡
```
~Binary_Search_Tree() { free_all_nodes(root); }
```

Most of these helper functions are friends rather than member functions, since they have no need to access the tree's data members; they work only with nodes. This is slightly more efficient, as there is no need to pass `this` as an extra, hidden parameter. Others, however, need to be member functions.

The `free_all_nodes` function uses a postorder traversal to free the child trees before releasing the root node. Since the traversal visits each node exactly once, its run-time efficiency (and, therefore, that of the destructor) is $O(n)$.

⟨Binary_Search_Tree *private function declarations* 81a⟩≡
```
friend void free_all_nodes(Node *root)
{
    if (root != nullptr) {
        free_all_nodes(root->lchild);
        free_all_nodes(root->rchild);
        delete root;
    }
}
```

The copy constructor also uses a recursive helper function, `copy_tree`, to do the actual copying. The new tree, of course, has the same number of nodes as the original. The `first` pointer must be initialized by traversing the tree from its root, but `cmp` need not be copied.

⟨Binary_Search_Tree *constructor declarations* 80b⟩+≡
```
Binary_Search_Tree(const
                      Binary_Search_Tree<T, Compare>& other)
{
    root = copy_tree(other.root);
    num_nodes = other.num_nodes;
    ⟨find first from root 81c⟩
}
```

The initial node in an inorder traversal (kept track of by the `first` pointer) can be found by following left child links as far as they can go from the root.

⟨*find* first *from* root 81c⟩≡
```
first = root;
if (first != nullptr) {
    while (first->lchild != nullptr) {
        first = first->lchild;
    }
}
```

We use a preorder traversal to copy the nodes in a tree. Note that by using a null default value for the `parent` parameter, the initial call to `copy_tree` (in chunk 81b) doesn't need to specify the—necessarily null—root parent pointer.

Like `free_all_nodes`, `copy_tree` visits each node once in its traversal, and therefore, is $O(n)$. Since the copying operation dominates the run-time of the copy constructor, it too is $O(n)$.

⟨Binary_Search_Tree *private function declarations* 81a⟩+≡

```
friend Node *copy_tree(Node *root, Node *parent = nullptr)
{
    if (root == nullptr) { return nullptr; }
    else {
        Node *result = new Node(root->data, parent);
        result->lchild = copy_tree(root->lchild, result);
        result->rchild = copy_tree(root->rchild, result);
        return result;
    }
}
```

The `initializer_list` constructor follows what will become a familiar pattern: using constructor forwarding to invoke the default constructor, and inserting each element of the initializer list as we iterate through it. Since each insertion is a $O(\log n)$ operation, and there are n insertions, the constructor is $O(n \log)$.

⟨Binary_Search_Tree *constructor declarations* 80b⟩+≡

```
Binary_Search_Tree(std::initializer_list<T> init)
    : Binary_Search_Tree()
{
    for (auto p = init.begin(); p != init.end(); p++) {
        insert(*p);
    }
}
```

The assignment operator is essentially the same as the copy constructor, except that it checks for (and ignores) attempts to assign a tree to itself and frees the nodes already used in the assignment target. Like the copy constructor, its run-time efficiency is $O(n)$.

⟨Binary_Search_Tree *constructor declarations* 80b⟩+≡

```
Binary_Search_Tree<T, Compare>& operator =
    (const Binary_Search_Tree<T, Compare>& other)
{
    if (this != other) {      // ignore assignment to self
        free_all_nodes(root);
        root = copy_tree(other.root);
        num_nodes = other.num_nodes;
        ⟨find first from root 81c⟩
    }
    return *this;
}
```

6.7.2 Member Functions

Accessors

The `size` and `empty` functions, as usual, are straightforward. The former simply returns the stored node count; the latter depends on `size`.

⟨Binary_Search_Tree *member function declarations* 83a⟩≡
```
int size() const { return num_nodes; }
bool empty() const { return size() == 0; }
```

The `count` member function makes use of a `search` helper function, which returns a pointer to the node containing the specified value (`item`) or the null pointer if it's not there. Since there are no duplicate values in the tree, an unsuccessful search gives the count of matching items as zero, a successful search as one.

⟨Binary_Search_Tree *member function declarations* 83a⟩+≡
```
int count(const T& item) const
{
    if (search(root, item) == nullptr) { return 0; }
    else { return 1; }
}
```

Because of `const` considerations not worth going into here, we need two versions of `search`: one `const` and one non-`const`. Fortunately, the C++ code for the body of both is identical. The non-`const` version uses pointer references rather than plain pointers so that it can be used in `erase` (see chunk 85a).

⟨Binary_Search_Tree *private function declarations* 81a⟩+≡
```
Node *search(Node *root, const T& x) const
     { ⟨use cmp to recursively search for x 83d⟩ }
Node *& search(Node *& root, const T& x)
     { ⟨use cmp to recursively search for x 83d⟩ }
```

Since the template only requires a less-than-like function, we can't assume that the '`==`' operator is defined for the element type. However, we can assume that if x ≮ root->data and x ≯ root->data, then it must be true that x = root->data. Otherwise, the code is an exact translation of the *search* algorithm in Section 6.3.

⟨use cmp *to recursively* search *for* x 83d⟩≡
```
if (root == nullptr) { return root; }
if (cmp(x, root->data)) {              // x < root->data
    return search(root->lchild, x);
} else if (cmp(root->data, x)) {       // x > root->data
    return search(root->rchild, x);
} else {                               // x = root->data
    return root;
}
```

To implement the **at** function for our **Map** class, we need to be able to find the node containing a value, so we implement a **find** function that returns an iterator specifying that node (or the **end** iterator if it doesn't exist). Once again, we need both **const** and non-**const** versions.

⟨Binary_Search_Tree *member function declarations* 83a⟩+≡

```
iterator find(const T& item)
    { return iterator(search(root, item)); }
const_iterator find(const T& item) const
    { return const_iterator(search(root, item)); }
```

Mutators

As with **count** and **find**, the **insert** function uses a recursive helper function, **add**, to do the real work. Unlike our **Set** and **Map** versions, we return an iterator specifying the newly inserted (or already existing) node. This is needed to implement the '**[]**' operator in our **Map** class.

⟨Binary_Search_Tree *member function declarations* 83a⟩+≡

```
iterator insert(const T& item)
    { return iterator(add(root, item)); }
```

Like **copy_tree**, the **add** function needs to keep track of which node should be the parent of the newly-added node, so we use a null default parameter to simplify the initial call using the tree's root. This code is a direct translation of the algorithm in Section 6.3, modified to return a pointer to the added node, to not assume the existence of an '**==**' operator for T, and to deal with parent pointers and the **first** and **num_nodes** data members.

⟨Binary_Search_Tree *private function declarations* 81a⟩+≡

```
Node *add(Node *& root, const T& x, Node *parent = nullptr)
{
    if (root == nullptr) {
        root = new Node(x, parent);
        ++num_nodes;
        if (first == nullptr
                or cmp(root->data, first->data)) {
            first = root;     // new node precedes current first
        }                     // in traversal
        return root;
    } else if (cmp(x, root->data)) {     // x < root->data
        return add(root->lchild, x, root);
    } else if (cmp(root->data, x)) {     // x > root->data
        return add(root->rchild, x, root);
    } else {                             // x = root->data
        // ignore duplicate insertions, but return node found
        return root;
    }
}
```

Since the non-`const` version of `search` returns a reference, there's no need to write a special helper function to traverse the tree to find the node to remove, but removing a node is non-trivial, so it makes sense to call a separate function, `remove_node`, to do this. We silently ignore attempts to remove a node with a value not in the tree.

⟨Binary_Search_Tree *member function declarations* 83a⟩+≡
```
void erase(const T& item)
{
    Node *& p = search(root, item);
    if (p != nullptr) {
        remove_node(p);
        --num_nodes;
    }
}
```

The `remove_node` function is a direct translation of the *remove_node* algorithm described in Section 6.3. The `curr` parameter should never be null, but it's simple enough (and safer) to ignore requests to remove a non-existent (null) node.

⟨Binary_Search_Tree *private function declarations* 81a⟩+≡
```
void remove_node(Node *& curr)
{
    if (curr == nullptr) { return; }    // defensive programming
    if (curr == first) { first = inorder_successor(curr); }
    if (curr->lchild == nullptr
            and curr->rchild == nullptr) {
        ⟨remove leaf node (case 1) 85c⟩
    } else if (curr->lchild == nullptr
            or curr->rchild == nullptr) {
        ⟨remove single-child node (case 2) 86a⟩
    } else {
        ⟨remove two-child node (case 3) 86b⟩
    }
}
```

We remove a leaf node by detaching it from its parent and freeing the space it used. Remember that `curr` is a reference parameter, so the assignment statement here sets the appropriate child pointer in the appropriate node (or `root` in a single-node tree) to the null pointer.

⟨remove leaf node (case 1) 85c⟩≡
```
delete curr;
curr = nullptr;
```

To remove a node that has only one child, we replace the current node with its child, and free the space used by the removed node. Again, using a reference parameter for `curr` simplifies the code by allowing us to assign it a new value.

⟨*remove single-child node (case 2)* 86a⟩≡

```
{
    Node *tmp = curr;
    if (curr->lchild != nullptr) { curr = curr->lchild; }
    else { curr = curr->rchild; }
    curr->parent = tmp->parent;
    delete tmp;
}
```

Removing a node with two children requires us to replace the node's **data** with that of its inorder successor and then remove the inorder successor node.

⟨*remove two-child node (case 3)* 86b⟩≡

```
{
    Node *successor = inorder_successor(curr);
    curr->data = successor->data;
    ⟨remove the successor node 86c⟩
}
```

We already know that the inorder successor must be either a leaf or a node with a single, right child, so we can safely call **remove_node** to remove it, knowing that we will recurse only one level.

The **if** statement is necessary because **remove_node** has to modify the appropriate child field in the parent node, but **inorder_successor** does not (and should not) return a reference. The **successor** of a node with two children cannot be the root node of the tree (the successor must be somewhere in the node's right subtree), so it must have a non-null parent.

⟨*remove the* successor *node* 86c⟩≡

```
if (successor == successor->parent->lchild) {
    remove_node(successor->parent->lchild);
} else {
    remove_node(successor->parent->rchild);
}
```

The **inorder_successor** function is a direct translation of the algorithm described in Section 6.3. As with **remove_node**, the **curr** parameter should never be null, but we check anyway. Note that a tree's root node has no inorder successor, so a null return value is perfectly valid (meaning that the node has no such successor).

⟨Binary_Search_Tree *private function declarations* 81a⟩+≡
```
  friend Node *inorder_successor(Node *curr)
  {
      if (curr == nullptr)      // defensive programming
          { return nullptr; }
      if (curr->rchild != nullptr) {
          ⟨slide curr down left from its right child 87b⟩
      } else {
          ⟨set curr to its first non-right-child ancestor 87c⟩
      }
      return curr;
  }
```

⟨*slide* curr *down left from its right child* 87b⟩≡
```
  curr = curr->rchild;
  while (curr->lchild != nullptr) {
      curr = curr->lchild;
  }
```

⟨*set* curr *to its first non-right-child ancestor* 87c⟩≡
```
  {
      Node *prev = curr;
      curr = curr->parent;
      while (curr != nullptr and prev == curr->rchild) {
          prev = curr;
          curr = curr->parent;
      }
  }
```

All we need to do to `clear` a tree is to free all the nodes, set all the pointers to null, and set the node count to zero.

⟨Binary_Search_Tree *member function declarations* 83a⟩+≡
```
  void clear()
  {
      free_all_nodes(root);
      root = first = nullptr;
      num_nodes = 0;
  }
```

6.7.3   Iterators

Except for the increment operators, which call `inorder_successor` instead of following a link, the code to implement `Binary_Search_Tree` iterators is exactly the same as that for `List`. It is fortuitous that the pointers to the initial `List` and `Binary_Search_Tree` nodes are both named `first`.

⟨Binary_Search_Tree<T>::Iter *operators* 88a⟩≡
```
  Iter<U>& operator ++()          // prefix ++
      { curr = inorder_successor(curr); return *this; }
  Iter<U> operator ++(int)        // postfix ++
  {
      Iter<U> result = Iter<U>(curr);
      curr = inorder_successor(curr);
      return result;
  }
```

⟨Binary_Search_Tree *helper classes* 80a⟩+≡
```
  template <typename U>
  class Iter {
  private:
      Node *curr;
      friend class Binary_Search_Tree<T>;
  public:
      Iter(Node *p) : curr(p) {}
```
      ⟨Binary_Search_Tree<T>::Iter *operators* 88a⟩
```
  };
```

⟨Binary_Search_Tree *type aliases* 88c⟩≡
```
  typedef Iter<T> iterator;
  typedef Iter<const T> const_iterator;
```

⟨Binary_Search_Tree<T>::Iter *operators* 88a⟩+≡
```
  U& operator *  () const { return curr->data; }
  U* operator -> () const { return &(curr->data); }
  bool operator == (const Iter& other) const
      { return curr == other.curr; }
  bool operator != (const Iter& other) const
      { return not(curr == other.curr); }
```

⟨Binary_Search_Tree *member function declarations* 83a⟩+≡
```
  iterator begin() { return iterator(first); }
  const_iterator begin() const
      { return const_iterator(first); }
```

⟨Binary_Search_Tree *member function declarations* 83a⟩+≡
```
  iterator end() { return iterator(nullptr); }
  const_iterator end() const
      { return const_iterator(nullptr); }
```

6.8 SET **AND** MAP **IMPLEMENTATION**

The Set and Map classes are both implemented using the Binary_-
Search_Tree class defined in Section 6.7. The class declaration for Set
mirrors that for Binary_Search_Tree almost exactly, with two template
parameters, T and Compare (the latter defaulting to less<T>), so we need
not show it here.

The Map declaration, however, is different enough to demand explanation. These differences all stem from the fact that the elements of a Map are
key-value pairs rather than single values. Instead of a single element type,
T, the Map template requires two types, K for the keys and V for the values.
Since the Compare function object type compares only keys, not values, we
have to provide a special cmp_func function object type that ignores the
second field in its comparisons (the default pair comparisons take both
fields into account).

⟨*interface for* Map 89⟩≡
```
    template <typename K, typename V,
              typename Compare = std::less<K> >
    class Map {
    private:
        ⟨Map's element_type definition 90a⟩
        struct cmp_func {
            Compare cmp;
            bool operator()(const element_type& a,
                            const element_type& b) const
                { return cmp(a.first, b.first); }
        };
    public:
        ⟨Map aliases 93b⟩
        ⟨Map functions 90e⟩
    private:
        ⟨Map data members 90c⟩
    };
```

The STL uses pair<const K, V> as the type for map elements, but
const issues make this difficult to do easily. In the interest of clarity and
simplicity, we define our own "workalike" class to do the job. The assignment operator with a const_cast is necessary to allow the assignment
statement in remove_node (chunk 86b) to work properly.

⟨Map's element_type *definition* 90a⟩≡
```
struct element_type {
    const K first;
    V second;
    element_type(const K& k, const V& v)
        : first(k), second(v) {}
    element_type& operator = (const element_type& other)
    {
        const_cast<K&>(first) = other.first;
        second = other.second;
        return *this;
    }
};
```

The Set and Map classes each have a single data member, tree, a Binary_Search_Tree. A Set tree's elements are the same as those specified for the Set, using the specified Compare function as well. A Map's tree contains key-value pairs (element_type) with our cmp_func function that compares only the keys.

⟨Set *data members* 90b⟩≡
```
Binary_Search_Tree<T, Compare> tree;
```

⟨Map *data members* 90c⟩≡
```
Binary_Search_Tree<element_type, cmp_func> tree;
```

6.8.1 Constructors/Destructors

Since the tree data member in each class does not explicitly use pointers, the compiler-generated destructors, copy constructors, and assignment operators are just fine. However, we do need to define initializer_list constructors, which pass the work along to the corresponding constructors from Binary_Search_Tree.

⟨Set *functions* 90d⟩≡
```
Set(std::initializer_list<T> init) : tree(init) {}
```

⟨Map *functions* 90e⟩≡
```
Map(std::initializer_list<element_type> init): tree(init) {}
```

We also have to define default constructors, because the C++ compiler does not generate one if any other constructors are defined. These constructors don't need to do anything, since the default Binary_Search_Tree constructor initializes the tree data member.

⟨Set *functions* 90d⟩+≡
```
Set() {}
```

⟨Map *functions* 90e⟩+≡
```
Map() {}
```

6.8.2 Member Functions

For the most part, the Set and Map member functions let the corresponding Binary_Search_Tree functions operate on tree.

Accessors

This is certainly the case for both the size and empty functions,

⟨Set *functions* 90d⟩+≡
```
int size() const { return tree.size(); }
bool empty() const { return tree.empty(); }
```

⟨Map *functions* 90e⟩+≡
```
int size() const { return tree.size(); }
bool empty() const { return tree.empty(); }
```

but Map's count function needs to look for a key-value pair, given only the key. Since our Map tree only uses the key part in comparisons, it's enough to pass a pair with a dummy value part.

⟨Set *functions* 90d⟩+≡
```
int count(const T& item) const { return tree.count(item); }
```

⟨Map *functions* 90e⟩+≡
```
int count(const K& key) const
    { return tree.count(element_type(key, V())); }
```

Map's '[]' operator inserts a default value if the specified element does not already exist. Since Binary_Search_Tree's insert function ignores duplicate insertions and the Map comparison function only compares keys, calling tree.insert with a (key, default-V value) pair does the job. A reference to the value part of the pair is returned (this is why Binary_Search_Tree's insert function returns an iterator instead of void).

⟨Map *functions* 90e⟩+≡
```
V& operator [] (const K& key)
{
    auto p = tree.insert(element_type(key, V()));
    return p->second;
}
```

No const version is necessary (or possible), since the insert operation may make changes to the tree.

The at function, on the other hand, needs a const version, but the code for both is the same, even though the const version returns a value while the non-const version returns a reference.

⟨Map *functions* 90e⟩+≡
```
V& at(const K& key)
{
    ⟨return value corresponding to key in this Map 92b⟩
}
V at(const K& key) const
{
    ⟨return value corresponding to key in this Map 92b⟩
}
```

The at function uses Binary_Search_Tree's find function to determine if a pair with the key exists in the tree. If so, it returns the value in the corresponding node (a reference to that value for the non-const version); if not, it throws an out_of_range exception.

⟨*return value corresponding to* key *in this* Map 92b⟩≡
```
auto p = tree.find(element_type(key, V()));
if (p == tree.end()) {
    throw std::out_of_range("nonexistent Map key");
}
return p->second;
```

Mutators

Only the Set class provides an insert function. It uses the corresponding Binary_Search_Tree function to do the real work.

⟨Set *functions* 90d⟩+≡
```
void insert(const T& item) { tree.insert(item); }
```

The clear and erase functions for both classes pass the job along to the corresponding Binary_Search_Tree function. The Map version uses a dummy pair with the given key and a meaningless value for erase (remember that only the key is used in searching a Map).

⟨Set *functions* 90d⟩+≡
```
void clear() { tree.clear(); }
void erase(const T& item) { tree.erase(item); }
```

⟨Map *functions* 90e⟩+≡
```
void clear() { tree.clear(); }
void erase(const K& key)
    { tree.erase(element_type(key, V())); }
```

6.8.3 Iterators

The Binary_Search_Tree iterators are sufficient in and of themselves, so we define the Set and Map iterators to be aliases. Since Set values cannot be modified (doing so might invalidate the tree's binary search property), only const iterators are supported for the Set class. Map has no such restriction, since the key part of each pair is itself const.

The "typename" keyword is required here because C++'s template mechanism cannot always determine when an identifier is the name of a template type. Such is the case here with Binary_Search_Tree.

⟨Set *aliases* 93a⟩≡
```
typedef typename
  Binary_Search_Tree<T,Compare>::const_iterator
    iterator;
typedef typename
  Binary_Search_Tree<T,Compare>::const_iterator
    const_iterator;
```

⟨Map *aliases* 93b⟩≡
```
typedef typename
  Binary_Search_Tree<element_type,cmp_func>::iterator
    iterator;
typedef typename
  Binary_Search_Tree<element_type,cmp_func>::const_iterator
    const_iterator;
```

The **begin** and **end** functions, therefore, need do no more than invoke tree.begin() and tree.end(), respectively.

⟨Set *functions* 90d⟩+≡
```
const_iterator begin() const { return tree.begin(); }
const_iterator end() const { return tree.end(); }
```

⟨Map *functions* 90e⟩+≡
```
      iterator begin()       { return tree.begin(); }
const_iterator begin() const { return tree.begin(); }
      iterator end()         { return tree.end(); }
const_iterator end() const { return tree.end(); }
```

PROGRAMMING EXERCISE

Write a function

```
Expr_Node* build_tree(queue<string>& expr);
```

that takes a queue of **string** tokens (**expr**) representing a valid infix expression, and returns the equivalent expression tree. You will need to adapt either the stack-based (from Chapter 4) or recursive-descent (from Chapter 5) infix-to-postfix algorithm to accomplish this. Use the following class declarations for the tree node types, and implement the **eval** member function for each of the concrete types, Value_Node, Plus_Node, Minus_Node, Times_Node, and Divide_Node. The lchild and rchild fields are declared "protected" in the Operation_Node class so that they can be accessed by the eval functions in its derived classes.

```cpp
class Expr_Node {
public:
    int eval() const = 0;
};

class Value_Node : public Expr_Node {
public:
    Value_Node(int value) : data(value) {}
    int eval() const;
private:
    int data;
};

class Operation_Node : public Expr_Node {
public:
    Operation_Node(Expr_Node *left, Expr_Node *right)

        : lchild(left), rchild(right) {}
protected:
    Expr_Node *lchild, *rchild;
};

class Plus_Node : public Operation_Node {
public:
    Plus_Node(Expr_Node *left, Expr_Node *right)
        : Operation_Node(left, right) {}
    int eval() const;
};

class Minus_Node : public Operation_Node {
public:
    Minus_Node(Expr_Node *left, Expr_Node *right)
        : Operation_Node(left, right) {}
    int eval() const;
};

class Times_Node : public Operation_Node {
public:
    Times_Node(Expr_Node *left, Expr_Node *right)
        : Operation_Node(left, right) {}
    int eval() const;
};

class Divide_Node : public Operation_Node {
public:
    Divide_Node(Expr_Node *left, Expr_Node *right)
        : Operation_Node(left, right) {}
    int eval() const;
};
```

CHAPTER 7

BINARY TREES (CONTINUED)

I t's no coincidence that the previous chapter is the longest in the book; the binary tree (and its variants) may very well be the most important component in a programmer's toolbox. This chapter serves as a kind of addendum, describing a few ways in which the basic ideas in the last chapter can be expanded or improved upon. It provides only a taste, however. There is plenty more you'll want to find out for yourself.

7.1 HEIGHT-BALANCED TREES

One problem with the basic binary search tree is that the efficiency of a search depends on the order in which items were inserted (or deleted). If items are inserted or deleted in an unfortunate order, the tree can become degenerate—in effect a linked list—and searching becomes linear rather than logarithmic. This is not much of a problem when the trees are small, but becomes significant as the number of nodes increases.

The solution, of course, is to find a way to keep the tree "balanced" after insertions and deletions. There are a number of techniques for doing this, the best known being *AVL trees* (named after their inventors, Georgii Adelson-Velsky and Evgenii Landis) and *red-black trees* (named after the colors "painted" on the nodes in order to maintain balance). Both of these trees guarantee logarithmic time for all operations. The algorithms are fairly complex, and won't be described here, but they are well-worth exploring when you have the time. AVL trees are slightly faster than red-black trees when searching, but red-black trees are slightly faster when it comes to inserting and deleting nodes.

The STL `set` and `map` clsetasses are implemented using red-black trees.

7.2 GENERAL TREES

You may have noticed that, for all the discussion of binary trees, no mention has been made of the possibility of more general trees, such as Figure 7.1, where a node is not limited to two children. One reason for this

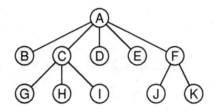

FIGURE 7.1 A general tree

is that a binary tree can be used to represent a general tree.

Recognizing that a degenerate binary tree is nothing more than a linked list provides the basis for such a representation. The left child pointer becomes a pointer to the node's first child, and the right child pointer becomes a pointer to the node's next sibling (creating a linked list of sibling nodes). Figure 7.2 shows the binary tree representation of Figure 7.1. Lisp-

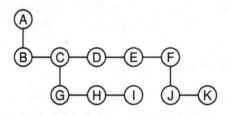

FIGURE 7.2 Binary tree representation of Figure 7.1

based programming languages rely on this technique.

7.3 HEAPS

A complete binary tree is called a *heap** when the value in each node is greater than the values of both its children. Figure 7.3 gives an example of one such tree. Another name for a heap is *priority queue.*

Because a heap is a complete tree, its height must be $\lfloor \log_2 n \rfloor$, which guarantees that insertion and removal operations are logarithmic. To insert a value (Figure 7.4), you create a new node containing the value and place

---

*Do not confuse this with the area of memory from which the new operator allocates storage, which is, unfortunately, called "the heap." The two concepts are completely unrelated.

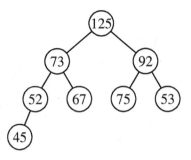

FIGURE 7.3 A binary tree heap

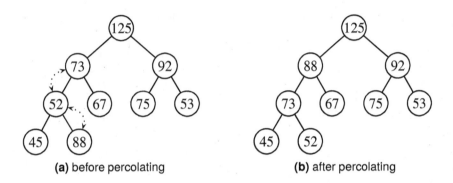

(a) before percolating   **(b)** after percolating

FIGURE 7.4 Inserting the value 88 into the tree in Figure 7.3

it in the next available position in the tree. Then you *percolate* the value up the tree to find its proper position. Since the percolation starts with a leaf at the tree's lowest level and traverses up toward the root, it visits at most one more node than the height of the tree. So insertion into a heap is $O(\log n)$.

To remove the root value (Figure 7.5; only the root value may be removed), you detach the last node added and put its value in the root node. You then percolate the value down the tree to find its proper position. Like insertion, the removal process visits at most one more node than the height of the tree, which means that removal is also $O(\log n)$.

Because a heap is a complete tree, it can be represented efficiently by an array or vector. The root node is at index 0, and for any node at index i, its left child is at index $2i + 1$; its right child at index $2i + 2$, and its parent is at index $\lfloor \frac{i-1}{2} \rfloor$. Figure 7.6 shows the tree in Figure 7.3 represented as a vector or array. This representation allows the insertion and removal algorithms to be easily expressed. Insertion involves extending the array/vector by one

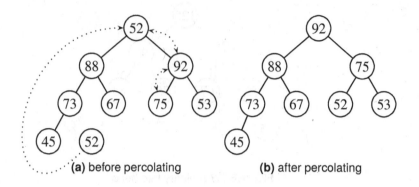

(a) before percolating   **(b)** after percolating

FIGURE 7.5 Removing the root value from the tree in Figure 7.4b

125	73	92	52	67	75	53	45
[0]	[1]	[2]	[3]	[4]	[5]	[6]	[7]

FIGURE 7.6 Array/vector representation of Figure 7.3

element, inserting the new value in it, and percolating the value up the tree.

> **Algorithm:** *heap_insert(h, n, x)*
> **Input:** *h*, a heap represented as an array or vector
> **Input:** *n*, the number of elements in the heap
> **Input:** *x*, the value to insert
>   expand *h* by one element
> $h[n] \leftarrow x$
>   *percolate_up(h, n + 1)*

The percolation is accomplished by comparing the new value to its parent's value (remember that the parent of a node at index *i* is at index $\lfloor \frac{i-1}{2} \rfloor$; integer division does the job of the floor function since *i* is never negative). If the parent's value is less than the child's, the values of the nodes are swapped. The process continues until either the root or a node whose value is less than its parent's is reached.

> **Algorithm:** *percolate_up(h, n)*
> **Input:** *h*, a heap represented as an array or vector
> **Input:** *n*, the number of elements in the heap
> $i \leftarrow n - 1$
> $p \leftarrow (i - 1) \div 2$
>   **while** $i > 0$ **and** $h[p] < h[i]$ **do**
>   *swap(h[p], h[i])*
> $i \leftarrow p$
> $p \leftarrow (i - 1) \div 2$

Removing the root involves replacing the root value with that of the last inserted node, which is then removed from the array/vector, and percolating the root value down the tree.

Algorithm: *heap_remove(h, n)*
Input: *h*, a heap represented as an array or vector
Input: *n*, the number of elements in the heap
 $h[0] \leftarrow h[n-1]$
 shrink *h* by one element
 percolate_down(h, n − 1)

The downward percolation is accomplished by comparing the root value to both of its children and swapping the value with its largest child. This process continues until a leaf or a node whose value is greater than that of both its children is reached.

Algorithm: *percolate_down(h, n)*
Input: *h*, a heap represented as an array or vector
Input: *n*, the number of elements in the heap
 $i \leftarrow 0$
 child ← *max_child(h, n, i)*
 while *child* < *n* **and** $h[i] < h[child]$ **do**
  swap(h[child], h[i])
  $i \leftarrow child$
  child ← *max_child(h, n, i)*

The two children of a node at index *p* are at indexes $2p + 1$ and $2p + 2$. The *max_child* algorithm assumes that the former contains the larger value of the two. If the latter exists in the array/vector and has a larger value, that assumption is corrected. In either case, the algorithm returns the appropriate index.

Algorithm: *max_child(h, n, p)*
Input: *h*, a heap represented as an array or vector
Input: *n*, the number of elements in the heap
Input: *p*, current position in the heap
Ouput: the position of the largest child of *p*
 result ← $2p + 1$
 if *result* + 1 < *n* **and** $h[result] < h[result + 1]$ **then**
  result ← *result* + 1
 return *result*

Figure 7.7 shows the value 88 inserted into the array/vector heap in Figure 7.6 (as in Figures 7.4/7.3), and Figure 7.8 shows the root value being removed from the resulting heap in Figure 7.7b (as in Figures 7.5/7.4b).

7.4 THE PRIORITY_QUEUE INTERFACE

Heaps are represented in the STL by the `priority_queue` class, defined in the <queue> header. Like the `stack` and `queue` classes, `priority_`

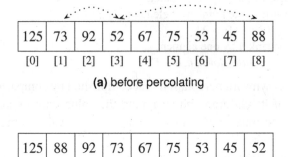

(a) before percolating

125	88	92	73	67	75	53	45	52
[0]	[1]	[2]	[3]	[4]	[5]	[6]	[7]	[8]

(b) after percolating

FIGURE 7.7 Inserting the value 88 into the tree in Figure 7.6

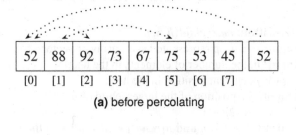

(a) before percolating

92	88	75	73	67	52	53	45
[0]	[1]	[2]	[3]	[4]	[5]	[6]	[7]

(b) after percolating

FIGURE 7.8 Removing the root value from the tree in Figure 7.7b

queue provides the usual size and empty functions, but does not provide iterators or a clear operation. The interface provides stack-like access to the heap elements.

Accessors

top	$O(1)$	root element

Mutators

push	$O(\log n)$	insert a new element
pop	$O(\log n)$	remove the root element

The push and pop operations run in logarithmic time; all other operations run in constant time.

7.5 PRIORITY_QUEUE IMPLEMENTATION

Unlike the STL, we provide our Priority_Queue class in its own header ("priority-queue.h"). Like the Set class, it needs a Compare parameter, which defaults to the standard less function class.

⟨*interface for* Priority_Queue 101a⟩≡
```
template <typename T, typename Compare = std::less<T> >
class Priority_Queue {
public:
    ⟨Priority_Queue member functions 102a⟩
private:
    ⟨Priority_Queue data members and private functions 101b⟩
};
```

The STL class actually has three template parameters, the second of which specifies which array-like data type is used to implement the heap. Thus, to use an STL priority_queue of integers sorted in reverse order, you would specify

```
priority_queue<int, vector<int>, greater<int> >
```

For simplicity, we define data to be a vector<T> (which is the STL's default), eliminating the second template parameter. As in our other binary tree classes, the cmp data member is defined to allow us to use the simpler function call syntax.

⟨Priority_Queue *data members and private functions* 101b⟩≡
```
std::vector<T> data;
Compare cmp;
```

7.5.1 Constructors/Destructors

We don't need any special constructors or destructor; the functions generated by the C++ compiler are sufficient.

7.5.2 Member Functions

Accessors

The `size` and `empty` functions pass their work along to the corresponding `vector` function,

⟨Priority_Queue *member functions* 102a⟩≡
```
    int size() const { return data.size(); }
    bool empty() const { return data.empty(); }
```

and the `top` element in the heap is always the first element in the `data` vector.

⟨Priority_Queue *member functions* 102a⟩+≡
```
    const T& top() const { return data.front(); }
```

Mutators

The insertion and removal functions are all direct translations of the algorithms in Section 7.3, with the `data` vector and the heap's `size` replacing the *h* and *n* parameters, respectively.

The *heap_insert* algorithm becomes the `push` function. The vector is expanded using `push_back`, of course.

⟨Priority_Queue *member functions* 102a⟩+≡
```
    void push(const T& item)
    {
        data.push_back(item);
        percolate_up();
    }
```

The `percolate_up` function is private, and a direct translation of the algorithm in Section 7.3.

⟨Priority_Queue *data members and private functions* 101b⟩+≡
```
    void percolate_up()
    {
        int i = size() - 1;
        int p = (i - 1) / 2;
        while (i > 0 and cmp(data[p], data[i])) {
            std::swap(data[p], data[i]);
            i = p;
            p = (i - 1) / 2;
        }
    }
```

The *heap_remove* algorithm becomes the `pop` function. We use calls to `data.front()` and `data.back()` because they are somewhat more descriptive than (and equivalent to) `data[0]` and `data[data.size()-1]`. The call to `data.pop_back()` removes the no-longer-needed element.

⟨Priority_Queue *member functions* 102a⟩+≡
```
void pop()
{
    data.front() = data.back();
    data.pop_back();
    percolate_down();
}
```

The private `percolate_down` and `max_child` functions are line-by-line translations of the corresponding algorithms, except that calls to the `cmp` "function" replace the less than operator with regard to `data` elements.

⟨Priority_Queue *data members and private functions* 101b⟩+≡
```
void percolate_down()
{
    int i = 0;
    int child = max_child(i);
    while (child < size() and cmp(data[i], data[child])) {
        std::swap(data[child], data[i]);
        i = child;
        child = max_child(i);
    }
}
int max_child(int p)
{
    int result = 2 * p + 1;
    if (result + 1 < size()
        and cmp(data[result], data[result + 1]))
    {
        ++result;
    }
    return result;
}
```

PROGRAMMING EXERCISE

Design and implement an `AVL_Tree` or `Red_Black_Tree` class, and use it instead of `Binary_Search_Tree` to implement the `Set` and `Map` classes.

Since this chapter doesn't include algorithms for AVL or red-black trees, you'll have to do a little research to find them.

CHAPTER 8

SORTING

S trictly speaking, sorting is not a data structures issue; the only data structure involved is an array. However, sorting is an important issue in computing, and the various algorithms provide excellent practice in algorithm analysis.

All the sorting algorithms in this chapter take two parameters, a, and n. The former is an array, the latter the number of elements in the array. Of course, a **vector** might be used in place of an array, in which case the second parameter is superfluous (the **size** member function supplies its value), and the first must be passed by reference (remember that in C++, an array is represented by a pointer to the first element so that, in essence, arrays are always passed by reference).

8.1 BUBBLE SORT (REVISED)

You've already seen an algorithm for a *bubble sort* (in Section 2.1.1), which uses nested loops to "bubble" the largest element to the end of the array, which contains an ever-growing collection of already-sorted values.

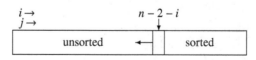

The inner loop compares every pair of elements from the first two up to the already sorted part of the array. Whenever the current element, $a[j]$ is found to be less than its successor, the values are swapped. In this way, the largest element is guaranteed to end up in the last unsorted location in the array, joining the sorted part.

You may have noticed that if the inner loop completes its iteration without having to swap any values, it means that the "unsorted" part of the array wasn't unsorted at all, and there's no need to continue. Modifying the algorithm to deal with this situation,

> **Algorithm:** *bubble_sort(a, n)*
> ──────────────────
> *done* ← *false*
> **for** *i* **from** 0 **to** *n* − 2 **while not** *done* **do**
>   *done* ← *true*
>   **for** *j* **from** 0 **to** *n* − 2 − *i* **do**
>   **if** *a*[*j* + 1] < *a*[*j*] **then**
>   swap the values of *a*[*j* + 1] and *a*[*j*]
>   *done* ← *false*

doesn't change the basic quadratic nature of the algorithm (the average and worst cases are still $O(n^2)$), but in the best case, when the array is already (or almost) completely sorted, only a few iterations of the inner loop are necessary, and the algorithm runs in linear time.

8.2 SELECTION SORT

Another simple sort algorithm is *selection sort*. In this algorithm, the already-sorted part is kept in the lower array elements.

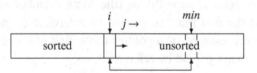

The *i* index always refers to the first unsorted position in the array. The *j* index scans through the unsorted elements, looking for the minimum value, which is then swapped with the value at index *i*. Since the minimum value must be larger than all of the already sorted values, and is (by definition) smaller than all the other unsorted values, this extends the sorted part of the array by one element.

> **Algorithm:** *selection_sort(a, n)*
> ──────────────────
> **for** *i* **from** 0 **to** *n* − 2 **do**
>   *min* ← *i*
>   **for** *j* **from** *i* + 1 **to** *n* − 1 **do**
>   **if** *a*[*j*] < *a*[*min*] **then** *min* ← *j*
>   swap the values of *a*[*i*] and *a*[*min*]

During the first iteration of the outer loop ($i = 0$), the inner loop executes its body $n - 1$ times. Each succeeding iteration of the inner loop executes its body one less time than the previous one, so the body of the inner loop executes a total of $(n - 1) + (n - 2) + \cdots + 3 + 2 + 1 = \frac{n(n-1)}{2}$ times, which means that selection sort, like bubble sort, is $O(n^2)$. However, the constant factors in bubble sort are significantly larger than those in selection sort, so the latter will always run faster than the former (except in the revised bubble sort's best case, where the array is already nearly or completely sorted).

8.3 INSERTION SORT

The last of the quadratic sorts is *insertion sort*, which is similar to the way that most people rearrange cards in a bridge or poker hand, inserting the cards one-by-one into their proper places.

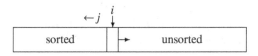

As in selection sort, i marks the place of the first unsorted element in the array. The sorted values greater than this value shift right to make space for it, whereupon the value is placed in its proper location, vacated by the last shift.

Algorithm: *insertion_sort(a, n)*
> **for** i **from** 0 **to** $n - 1$ **do**
>> $tmp \leftarrow a[i]$
>> $j \leftarrow i - 1$
>> **while** $j \geq 0$ **and** $tmp < a[j]$ **do**
>>> $a[j + 1] \leftarrow a[j]$
>>> $j \leftarrow j - 1$
>> $a[j + 1] \leftarrow tmp$

Since the inner loop scans for the first value less than the current one, it does nothing when that value is greater than the largest already sorted value, so in the best case (when the array is already sorted), the algorithm is $O(n)$. However, in the worst case (when the values are in reverse order), the inner loop body executes $(n - 1) + (n - 2) + \cdots + 3 + 2 + 1$ times, just like the inner loop of selection sort, and is thus $O(n^2)$. On average, too, the run-time of insertion sort is also $O(n^2)$.

Since the inner loop does nothing when a value is already in its proper place, and the overhead factors in the algorithm are also significantly smaller than those in selection or bubble sort, insertion sort is the fastest of the $O(n^2)$ sorts.

8.4 SHELL SORT

There are sorting algorithms that are better than quadratic, however, and these are much preferable to the $O(n^2)$ algorithms. The first of these is *shell sort*, which is named after its designer, Donald L. Shell. Shell sort is similar to bubble sort in that it involves comparing elements and swapping them when they are out of place. Unlike bubble sort, shell sort does not compare adjacent elements until the last iteration. Instead, it first compares elements that are widely separated, shrinking the size of the gap with each pass. In this way, it deals with elements that are grossly out of place early on, reducing the amount of work that later passes must do.

Algorithm: *shell_sort(a, n)*

$gap \leftarrow n \div 2$
while $gap > 0$ **do**
  for i **from** gap **to** $n - 1$ **do**
    $j \leftarrow i - gap$
    while $j \geq 0$ **and** $a[j] > a[j + gap]$ **do**
      swap the values of $a[j]$ and $a[j + gap]$
      $j \leftarrow j - gap$
  $gap \leftarrow gap \div 2$

The analysis of shell sort is rather complicated. It's enough to know that shell sort has a run-time efficiency of $O(n^{1.5})$ (or, equivalently, $O(n\sqrt{n})$).

8.5 HEAP SORT

The idea for *heap sort* comes from the efficient implementation of a heap as an array and the knowledge that insertion and removal from a heap are $O(\log n)$ operations. The *percolate_up* algorithm (Section 7.3) is used to create successively larger heaps (starting with a size of 2, since a single element array is trivially a heap), ending up with the whole array as an n-element heap.

At this point, the heap property ensures that the largest element in the array is in the first element, so swapping it with the value in the last element puts it in its proper place. The situation is now the same as when a heap's root element has been removed and replaced with the last leaf element. The *percolate_down* algorithm (Section 7.3) restores the heap property for the now $(n-1)$-element heap, and the process repeats until the heap has shrunk to a single element, and the whole array is sorted.

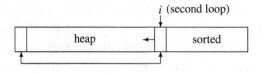

Algorithm: *heap_sort(a, n)*

> **for** *i* **from** 2 to *n* **do**
>> *percolate_up(a, i)*
>
> **for** *i* **from** *n* − 1 **down to** 1 **do**
>> swap the values of *a*[0] and *a*[*i*]
>> *percolate_down(a, i)*

Since both percolate algorithms are $O(\log n)$ and both loops iterate $n - 1$ times, the loops are each $O(n \log n)$, and since they are consecutive rather than nested, the whole algorithm is $O(n \log n)$.

In fact, $O(n \log n)$ is the theoretical speed limit for comparison-based sorting algorithms. However, heap sort is not the fastest of these, as you will see.

8.6 MERGE SORT

Unlike the previous sort algorithms, *merge sort* is recursive, and as is often the case with recursive algorithms, is best handled by a "helper" algorithm with extra parameters. In this case, the extra parameters specify the indexes of the first and last elements of a range to be sorted. Initially, of course, the range is from the first (index 0) through the last element (index $n - 1$).

Algorithm: *merge_sort(a, n)*

> *msort(a, 0, n − 1)*

Merge sort is a *divide-and-conquer* algorithm. Simply put, it divides the range to be sorted into two equal halves, recursively sorts both halves, then merges the two sorted halves back into the specified range. It's possible to do this without using a second, temporary array to hold the merged values, but this way is easier to explain (and understand).

Algorithm: *msort(a, start, stop)*

> **if** *start* < *stop* **then**   *// size* ≤ 1 $\implies$ already sorted
>> *// sort left and right halves separately*
>> *mid* ← (*start* + *stop*) ÷ 2
>> *msort(a, start, mid)*
>> *msort(a, mid + 1, stop)*
>> construct temp. array, *b*, with *stop* − *start* + 1 elements
>> ⟨merge left and right halves into *b*⟩
>> copy contents of *b* back into *a*[*start*] through *a*[*stop*]

Merging the two halves is a straightforward process. Two variables, pos_{left} and pos_{right}, keep track of the current position (initially the first) in each of the halves and a third, pos_b, keeps track of the current position (initially the first) in the temporary array, *b*.

The loop copies the smaller of the values $a[pos_{left}]$ and $a[pos_{right}]$ into the next available position in b, continuing until all the values in one or both of the halves have been copied to b. Since the two halves are already sorted, the smaller of the values at the current positions must be the smallest value not already merged.

⟨merge left and right halves into b⟩≡
$pos_b \leftarrow 0$; $pos_{left} \leftarrow start$; $pos_{right} \leftarrow mid + 1$
while $pos_{left} \leq mid$ **and** $pos_{right} \leq stop$ **do**
  if $a[pos_{left}] < a[pos_{right}]$ **then**
    $b[pos_b] \leftarrow a[pos_{left}]$
    $pos_{left} \leftarrow pos_{left} + 1$
  else
    $b[pos_b] \leftarrow a[pos_{right}]$
    $pos_{right} \leftarrow pos_{right} + 1$
  $pos_b \leftarrow pos_b + 1$
⟨copy excess elements (if any) into b⟩

When the loop ends, there will still be values to be copied, either in the left or right half of the range (but not both—one of the halves must have been completely copied or the loop wouldn't have ended). If $pos_{left} \leq mid$, there are unmerged values in the left half; if $pos_{right} \leq stop$, the unmerged values are in the right half. These "excess" values must all be larger than the already merged ones, so they just need to be copied to the remaining slots in b. Since only one of the conditions can be true, only one of the loops will actually do anything.

⟨copy excess elements (if any) into b⟩≡
  // copy excess left-half elements (if any) into b
  while $pos_{left} \leq mid$ **do**
    $b[pos_b] \leftarrow a[pos_{left}]$
    $pos_{left} \leftarrow pos_{left} + 1$
    $pos_b \leftarrow pos_b + 1$
  // copy excess right-half elements (if any) into b
  while $pos_{right} \leq stop$ **do**
    $b[pos_b] \leftarrow a[pos_{right}]$
    $pos_{right} \leftarrow pos_{right} + 1$
    $pos_b \leftarrow pos_b + 1$

Each recursive call splits the array exactly in half, to a depth of $\log_2 n$, each of which does $O(n)$ work. This makes the merge sort $O(n \log n)$ in all cases. Unlike the other sorts in this chapter, which have no extra memory requirements (and are therefore $O(1)$ in that regard), merge sort requires $O(n)$ extra space for the merges. However, even though merge sort is more complex than heap sort, its constant factors are actually smaller, so merge sort is consistently faster than heap sort.

8.7 QUICK SORT

Quick sort is another recursive, divide-and-conquer algorithm, and like merge sort, uses a helper whose parameters specify the range of elements to be sorted, initially the whole array.

Algorithm: *quick_sort(a, n)*
qsort(a, 0, n − 1)

The quick sort algorithm is almost trivial in its simplicity. The range being sorted is partitioned into two parts, around a *pivot* value, where every element in the left partition is less than or equal to the pivot value and every element in the right partition is greater than the pivot value. The algorithm is then called recursively to sort each of the partitions (the pivot value is already in its proper place).

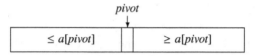

Algorithm: *qsort(a, start, stop)*
if *start* < *stop* **then**   // size ≤ 1 ⟹ already sorted
    pivot ← *partition(a, start, stop)*
    qsort(a, start, pivot − 1)
    qsort(a, pivot + 1, stop)

The efficiency of quick sort depends on the quality of the partition algorithm, which must be $O(n)$. A perfect partition algorithm will always split the range into equal halves, and therefore has a recursive depth of $\log_2 n$, and a best case efficiency of $O(n \log n)$. On average, quick sort is also $O(n \log n)$.

Unfortunately, there's no such thing as a perfect partition algorithm. In the worst case, the pivot value is the smallest or largest in the range, so that one partition is empty and the other is one element shorter than the range as a whole. If the values in the array happen to be arranged in such a way that the partition algorithm always produces the worst case, the depth of recursion becomes $O(n)$ instead of $O(\log n)$, and quick sort has a worst case efficiency of $O(n^2)$.

A simple partitioning strategy is to choose whatever value is first in the range as the pivot, swapping the smaller values to the left, as necessary, and moving the pivot value to its proper position (as determined by the swapping). It's easy to see that this partitioning algorithm produces worst case behavior when applied to an already sorted array.

Algorithm: *partition*(*a*, *start*, *stop*)

> *pivot* ← *start*
> *pivot_value* ← *a*[*pivot*]
> **for** *i* **from** *start* + 1 **to** *stop* **do**
>   **if** *a*[*i*] < *pivot_value* **then**
>   *pivot* ← *pivot* + 1
>   swap the values of *a*[*pivot*] and *a*[*i*]
>   swap the values of *a*[*pivot*] and *a*[*start*]
> **return** *pivot*

Even though it can't guarantee $O(n \log n)$ behavior, quick sort is almost always faster than any other sorting algorithm. There are a number of techniques for avoiding worst case behavior. The pivot value can be chosen as the range's middle element, a random element, or the median of three values. None of these can guarantee against bad partitioning, but the last seems to work well in practice.

It seems counterintuitive, but for small values of *n*, insertion sort is actually faster than quick sort (the partitioning overhead takes more time than is saved by the logarithmic divide-and-conquer). The efficiency of quick sort can therefore be improved by using insertion sort when the size of a range falls below a certain threshold.

Unlike merge sort, the quick sort algorithm is tail recursive, so the second call can be eliminated (either by hand or optimizing compiler). If you modify the algorithm so that the first recursive call always sorts the smaller partition, you remove any potential problem with regard to the depth of worst case recursion (but not the $O(n^2)$ behavior).

8.8 THE STL SORT FUNCTION

The STL provides a `sort` function, so you don't have to write your own. This function is guaranteed to be $O(n \log n)$, even in the worst case, but the standard does not specify any particular algorithm. It is usually implemented as a combination of quick and heap sorts, with the latter used only when the recursion gets too deep because of unfortunate partitioning. This "hybrid" algorithm is sometimes referred to as an *introspective sort*.

The function requires two iterator parameters, specifying the start and end of the range to be sorted. For example, if v is a `vector`, the call

```
std::sort(v.begin(), v.end());
```

sorts the contents of the entire vector. Since pointers are a special kind of iterator, the standard `sort` function can also be used to sort arrays. If a is an array with *n* elements, the call

```
std::sort(a, a + n);
```

sorts the entire array.

The **sort** function has an optional third parameter, the name of a **bool** function that compares two values, to be used instead of a simple "less than" comparison. If the function **func** is defined as

```
template <typename T>
bool func(const T& a, const T& b)
{
    return a > b;
}
```

then the call

```
std::sort(v.begin(), v.end(), func);
```

sorts **v** in descending rather than ascending order, assuming that the '>' operator is defined for **v**'s base type.

PROGRAMMING EXERCISE

Implement each of the sort algorithms in this chapter as C++ functions. You may use an STL **vector** parameter instead of an array and its size, if you wish. Receive extra credit for implementing them as template functions,

```
template <typename T, typename Compare = std::less<T>>
```

which can work with any base type or comparison function (using the standard less than operation by default for the latter).

CHAPTER 9

HASH TABLES

A *hash table* is a data structure with the unusual property that all accesses—insertion, deletion, and search—run in constant time. The trade-off is that there is no longer any natural order to the elements, which means that an iteration through the elements may access them in any order.

Hash tables are basically arrays, each element of which is called a *bucket*, combined with a *hash function, h(x)*, that takes a value and converts it into an integer. Figure 9.1 shows a table with 10 buckets that uses a simplistic

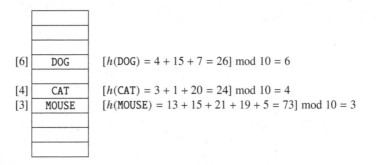

FIGURE 9.1 10-Bucket hash table

hash function, adding up the letters in a word, with 'A' = 1, 'B' = 2, and so on. The hash value of each item in the table is reduced (via mod) to the size of the table to determine the bucket in which the item is to be placed.

9.1 HASH FUNCTIONS

The quality of the hash function is vital to the efficiency of the table. A good hash function distributes its return values evenly over the allowable integers, and runs in constant time. Similar input values should have widely differing outputs. Needless to say, the hash function used in Figure 9.1 is a particularly poor one (but it's easy to compute, so it's good for examples).

Designing a good hash function for a set of possible values is not easy to do. Fortunately, the C++11 standard library provides (in the `<functional>` header) the `hash<T>` function object class with implementations for all of the types you're likely to need one for (`hash<int>`, `hash<string>`, etc.). You may, of course, define your own.

When all the items to be placed in a table are known in advance (as in a list of reserved words for a programming language), it is possible to create a *perfect hash function*, which for n distinct values, produces n distinct outputs in the range 0 through $n - 1$, so that each item hashes to a unique bucket. Unfortunately, the items placed in a hash table are rarely known in advance, so imperfect hash functions must be dealt with.

9.2 COLLISIONS

Suppose you want to add the value 'GERBIL' to the table in Figure 9.1. You compute the hash value $h(\text{GERBIL}) = 7 + 5 + 18 + 2 + 9 + 12 = 53$. But 53 mod 10 = 3, and bucket 3 is already occupied by 'MOUSE'. This is called a *collision*. There are two basic techniques for dealing with collisions: *probing* and *chaining*.

9.2.1 Probing

Probing involves looking for an empty bucket in a well-defined manner, starting at the computed hash value. The simplest of these techniques is *linear probing*, where the buckets are probed sequentially. Figure 9.2a shows 'GERBIL' inserted into the Figure 9.1 table using linear probing. Bucket 3 is occupied by 'MOUSE', so bucket 4 is checked. Since bucket 4 is also occupied (by 'CAT'), but bucket 5 is unoccupied, 'GERBIL' goes into bucket 5. To find an item in a linear probed table, it's not enough to just check the bucket indicated by the hash value; you must continue probing until you find either an empty bucket or one containing the item. Unfortunately, this makes it possible for items with different hash values to be part of the same probing sequence. For example, to next add PUPPY (hash value $16 + 21 + 16 + 16 + 25 = 94$) to the table in Figure 9.2a, you would probe buckets 4, 5, and 6 (all occupied) before finding that bucket 7 is free, even though these buckets represent items from three different probing

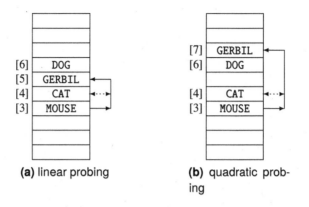

(a) linear probing   (b) quadratic probing

FIGURE 9.2 Inserting GERBIL in the Figure 9.1 table using probing

sequences. This intermingling of items with different hash values causes values to cluster, and increases the amount of time needed to find an item in the table.

Quadratic probing is similar to linear probing in that the first bucket probed after the initial collision is the next one in sequence. However, if a second probe is necessary, it goes to the fourth bucket after the initial one; a third probe checks the ninth bucket after the initial one; and so on. In general, the i-th probe for an item with hash value $h(x)$ in a table with b buckets is at bucket $(h(x) + i^2)$ mod b. Figure 9.2b shows 'GERBIL' inserted into the Figure 9.1 table using quadratic probing. Instead of probing bucket 5 after finding 4 occupied, the second probe goes to bucket 7 $((53 + 2^2 = 53 + 4 = 57)$ mod 10). If bucket 7 had been occupied, the next probe would have been to bucket $(53 + 3^2 = 53 + 9 = 61)$ mod 10 = 1. The fact that successive probes are further apart than the initial ones makes clustering less likely than in linear probing, but it does not eliminate the problem.

Another disadvantage of probing is the difficulty of removing items from the table while maintaining the integrity of the various probing sequences (see the programming exercise at the end of the chapter).

9.2.2 Chaining

A solution to the problems of probing is *chaining*. In a chained hash table, each bucket is a linked list ("chain") rather than a single value. Each linked list contains all the items having a hash value that corresponds to its bucket number. Collisions are resolved by adding the colliding items to the appropriate list. Figure 9.3 shows a chained table corresponding to the tables in Figure 9.2. Searching for an item involves sequentially searching

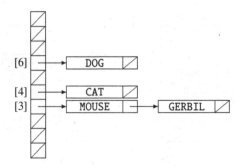

FIGURE 9.3 Inserting GERBIL in the Figure 9.1 table using chaining

(probing) the list corresponding to the item's hash value. Removing an item (once found) involves removing it from the list in its bucket.

Given a reasonable hash function, the chains are usually short, and unlike probing sequences, never interfere with each other. This, plus the fact that item removal is easy to implement, makes chaining the implementation method of choice for hash tables.

9.3 LOAD FACTORS AND EFFICIENCY

The ratio of the number of items in the table to the number of buckets is called the *load factor*, and is designated by the Greek letter α. The ultimate efficiency of a hash table implementation depends on the hash function, the collision resolution method, and the table's load factor. It's fairly safe to assume a good hash function; it's the other two factors that vary.

Obviously, because of collisions, hash table searches cannot always take constant time. Table 9.1 shows the average number of probes to be expected

α	Linear Probing	Quadratic Probing	Chaining
10%	1.06	1.05	1.05
25%	1.17	1.15	1.12
50%	1.50	1.39	1.25
60%	1.75	1.53	1.30
75%	2.50	1.85	1.38
80%	3.00	2.00	1.40
90%	5.50	2.56	1.45
99%	50.5	4.65	1.50

TABLE 9.1 Average number of probes for successful hash table search

for each combination of these factors. As you can see, a 50 percent loaded linear probed table, a 60 percent loaded quadratic probed table, and a 99 percent loaded chained table can all expect about one and a half probes for each successful search. Since each probe takes a constant amount of time, successful searches amortize to $O(1)$.

Unsuccessful searches generally require more probes than successful ones, particularly when using linear or quadratic probing on an almost full table. For 50 percent loaded linear probed and quadratic probed tables, the average number of probes is 2.5 and 2, respectively, while an unsuccessful search in a chained table with a 99 percent load factor averages only 1.79 probes. Again, in these cases, the searches amortize to $O(1)$.

For all of these, the worst case, when all the table items hash to the same bucket (which can happen even with a good hash function, when the input data is particularly perverse), is $O(n)$, since all the items must be probed to find the correct one.

Memory requirements are comparable for each of these techniques. Even though linked lists require extra space for the links, a chained table still works quite well when almost completely full, whereas the probed tables need to leave about half of their buckets empty.

9.4 REHASHING

In order to keep the average number of probes low (and the efficiency at $O(1)$), an optimal load factor must be maintained. For linear and quadratic probed tables, 50 percent and 60 percent are reasonable values, respectively; for a chained table, a 100 percent load factor is reasonable (note that it is possible for a chained table to have a load factor greater than 100 percent). When an insertion causes a hash table's load factor to exceed its optimal load factor, the table should be *rehashed*. Rehashing involves increasing the number of buckets, recomputing the hash values for each of the items, and relocating the items to the appropriate buckets in the new-sized table. Even though rehashing is a $O(n)$ operation, it should not occur very often, and does not affect the average $O(1)$ efficiency of the insertion operation.

9.5 THE UNORDERED_SET AND UNORDERED_MAP INTERFACES

Hash tables are represented in the STL by the `unordered_set` and the `unordered_map` classes. These classes were introduced in C++11 and are not available in earlier versions of the standard. These classes provide the same functionality as the `set` and `map` classes, but they are implemented using hash tables instead of binary search trees.

The **unordered** classes provide the same operations as **set** and **map**, but what were $O(\log n)$ functions are now $O(1)$. In addition, both classes provide the following functions:

Accessors

`load_factor`	$O(1)$	the current load factor
`max_load_factor`	$O(1)$	the maximum load factor; an automatic rehash occurs when this is exceeded

Mutators

`max_load_factor`	$O(1)$	change the maximum load factor value
`rehash`	$O(n)$	regenerate the hash table with at least the specified number of buckets

The default maximum load factor value is 1.0 (100 percent .

9.6 A HASH_TABLE **CLASS**

Since the STL's **unordered_set** and **unordered_map** classes are based on hash tables, just as **set** and **map** are based on binary search trees, it's not surprising that our implementations of **Unordered_Set** and **Unordered_Map** use a **Hash_Table** class as a basis.

Our **Hash_Table** class implementation follows the same pattern as the **Binary_Search_Tree** class defined in Section 6.7. However, instead of the comparison function needed by **Binary_Search_Tree**, it needs template arguments for the hash and equality functions to be used in probing. By default, we use the standard **hash<T>** for the former and **equal_to<T>** for the latter.

⟨*interface for* Hash_Table 120⟩≡
```
    template <typename T, typename H = std::hash<T>,
                          typename Equal = std::equal_to<T> >
    class Hash_Table {
    private:
        ⟨Hash_Table helper classes 126a⟩
    public:
        ⟨Hash_Table type aliases 126b⟩
        ⟨Hash_Table constructor declarations 121d⟩
        ⟨Hash_Table member function declarations 122a⟩
    private:
        ⟨Hash_Table data members 121a⟩
    };
```

We use the chaining technique for collision resolution, so each bucket in `table` is a linked list of items, and we keep track of the total number of items in the table (`num_elements`) to ensure that the `size` function is $O(1)$.

⟨Hash_Table *data members* 121a⟩≡
```
std::vector< std::list<T> > table;
int num_elements;
```

As usual, we provide function object data members (`hash` and `eq`) to simplify the syntax of these function calls.

⟨Hash_Table *data members* 121a⟩+≡
```
H hash;
Equal eq;
```

We also need to keep track of the maximum allowable load factor, so we'll know when an insertion triggers a rehash.

⟨Hash_Table *data members* 121a⟩+≡
```
float load_factor_limit;
```

9.6.1 Constructors/Destructors

The default constructor builds an empty hash table with a single bucket and a maximum load factor of 100 percent but a user may specify a different initial number of buckets.

⟨Hash_Table *constructor declarations* 121d⟩≡
```
Hash_Table(int num_buckets = 1)
    : table(num_buckets | 0x1),
      num_elements(0),
      load_factor_limit(1.0)
{}
```

Ideally, a prime number of buckets helps reduce the number of collisions, and most STL implementations keep a list of precomputed primes to ensure this. For our purposes, however, it's good enough to have an odd number of buckets. The '`| 0x1`' operation in the initialization of `table` sets the least significant bit of the value, thus guaranteeing an odd number of buckets.

The `initializer_list` constructor builds a table with just enough buckets to hold the items in the list.

⟨Hash_Table *constructor declarations* 121d⟩+≡
```
Hash_Table(std::initializer_list<T> init)
    : Hash_Table(init.size())
{
    for (auto p = init.begin(); p != init.end(); p++) {
        insert(*p);
    }
}
```

The destructor and other constructors generated by the compiler are sufficient.

9.6.2 Member Functions

Accessors

We use the usual implementations of `size` and `empty`.

⟨Hash_Table *member function declarations* 122a⟩≡
```
int size() const { return num_elements; }
bool empty() const { return size() == 0; }
```

As in `Binary_Search_Tree`, the `count` function performs a search for the specified item, returning zero if it's not found or one if it is. The `find` function (needed to implement `Unordered_Map`'s `at` function) does the searching.

⟨Hash_Table *member function declarations* 122a⟩+≡
```
int count(const T& item) const
{
    if (find(item) == end()) { return 0; }
    else { return 1; }
}
```

Both `const` and non-`const` versions of `find` are needed, but typically, they share the same code. This function returns an iterator referring to the value found if it's successful, `end()` if it's not.

⟨Hash_Table *member function declarations* 122a⟩+≡
```
iterator find(const T& item)
    { ⟨find item in the table and return iterator pointing to it 123a⟩ }
const_iterator find(const T& item) const
    { ⟨find item in the table and return iterator pointing to it 123a⟩ }
```

An `item` is in a table if and only if it is an element of the list in the appropriate bucket. We iterate through the list, returning the appropriate iterator if the value is found. If the loop ends without finding it, we return `end()`, indicating that `item` is not in the table. The template-specified `eq` function determines whether or not `item` is equal to a list element.

Iterators for the `vector` class are what is known as *random access iterators*. These iterators allow pointer-like "address arithmetic"; the expression "`table.begin() + b`" designates the iterator that refers to the `vector` element `table[b]`.

⟨*find* item *in the table and return iterator pointing to it* 123a⟩≡
```
    {
        ⟨compute b, the index of the bucket to use for item 123b⟩
        for (auto p = table[b].begin(); p != table[b].end();
                p++) {
            if (eq(*p, item)) {
                decltype(find(item))
                    result(table.begin() + b, table.end(), p);
                return result;
            }
        }
        return end();
    }
```

The decltype keyword is a C++11 construct that allows a programmer to specify that a variable is the same type as a given expression. In this case, result is declared to be the same type as find's return type, which means that it is an iterator in the non-const version of find, but a const_iterator in the const version.

The hash function (modulo the number of buckets) determines which bucket to use. Unfortunately, C++'s '%' operator does not implement the mathematical mod function; it fails when the hash function returns a negative value. In this case, we have $-$table.size() $< b <$ 0, and adding table.size() to b produces the correct result.

⟨*compute b, the index of the bucket to use for* item 123b⟩≡
```
    int b = hash(item) % table.size();
    if (b < 0) { b += table.size(); }
```

The load factor, α, is defined as $\frac{\text{number of elements}}{\text{number of buckets}}$, so that's just what we return for the load_factor function. Since both values are integral, we convert them to float for the computation.

⟨Hash_Table *member function declarations* 122a⟩+≡
```
    float load_factor() const
        { return float(num_elements) / float(table.size()); }
```

The max_load_factor accessor function reports the remembered value in load_factor_limit.

⟨Hash_Table *member function declarations* 122a⟩+≡
```
    float max_load_factor() const { return load_factor_limit; }
```

Mutators

As in Binary_Search_Tree, the insert function returns an iterator so that it can be used in the implementation of Unordered_Map's '[]' operator. If we find item in the appropriate bucket, we immediately return an iterator referring to its location. Otherwise, we add it to to the list and then return the iterator.

⟨Hash_Table *member function declarations* 122a⟩+≡
```
    iterator insert(const T& item)
    {
        ⟨compute b, the index of the bucket to use for item 123b⟩
        for (auto p = table[b].begin(); p != table[b].end();
                p++) {
            if (eq(*p, item)) {
                return iterator(table.begin() + b,
                                table.end(), p);
            }
        }
        ⟨add item to the list in bucket b, providing iterator p 124b⟩
        return iterator(table.begin() + b, table.end(), p);

    }
```

We use `list::insert` to add `item` to the end of the appropriate bucket, and note that the table now has another element. If the insertion causes the load factor to grow too large, we rehash the table to twice its previous number of buckets (plus one to keep the number odd). Since rehashing creates a whole new collection of buckets, the `list` iterator p is no longer valid, and we have to use `find` to locate where its value has been relocated.

⟨add item *to the list in bucket* b, *providing iterator* p 124b⟩≡
```
    auto p = table[b].insert(table[b].end(), item);
    ++num_elements;
    if (load_factor() > max_load_factor()) {
        rehash(2 * table.size() + 1);
        return find(item);
    }
```

To remove an `item` from a table, we use `find` to get an iterator locating it. If the value is actually in the table, we remove it from its bucket and note that we have one less element in the table. If `item` is not in the table, we quietly ignore the request.

⟨Hash_Table *member function declarations* 122a⟩+≡
```
    void erase(const T& item)
    {
        iterator p = find(item);
        if (p != end()) {
            p.bucket->erase(p.curr);
            --num_elements;
        }
    }
```

The `max_load_factor` mutator modifies the `load_factor_limit` data member, but does not rehash the table, even if this new limit is exceeded by the current load factor.

⟨Hash_Table *member function declarations* 122a⟩+≡
```
void max_load_factor(float new_limit)
{
    load_factor_limit = new_limit;
}
```

We rehash a table by constructing a new vector with the appropriate number of buckets. If the specified number of buckets would cause the load factor to be greater than the allowed maximum, the new vector will have just enough buckets to keep the load factor within bounds.

We use the **vector::swap** member function (which hasn't been mentioned before, but which swaps the contents of two vectors in constant time) to replace the **table** data member with the new vector, after which we go through the contents of the old table and insert each value into the new table.

⟨Hash_Table *member function declarations* 122a⟩+≡
```
void rehash(int num_buckets)
{
    num_buckets = std::max(num_buckets,
                        int(ceil(float(size())
                            / max_load_factor()))) | 0x1;
    std::vector< std::list<T> > v(num_buckets);
    table.swap(v);
    num_elements = 0;
    for (auto p = v.begin(); p != v.end(); p++) {
        for (auto q = p->begin(); q != p->end(); q++) {
            insert(*q);
        }
    }
}
```

To clear a hash table, we clear all the buckets and set the element count to zero. The number of buckets remains the same.

⟨Hash_Table *member function declarations* 122a⟩+≡
```
void clear()
{
    for (auto p = table.begin(); p != table.end(); p++) {
        p->clear();
    }
    num_elements = 0;
}
```

9.6.3 Iterators

Because of **const** considerations, our **Iter** template requires two extra template parameters. A **Hash_Table** iterator needs to keep track of two things: the current **bucket**, and the current element within that bucket (curr). These two parameters supply the actual iterator (or const_iterator) types of these data members. The bucket iterator also needs to know when bucket has gone past the end of the table. This is the job of the table_end data member.

⟨Hash_Table *helper classes* 126a⟩≡
```
    template <typename U, typename It1, typename It2>
    class Iter {
    private:
        It1 bucket, table_end;
        It2 curr;
        friend class Hash_Table;
    public:
        Iter(const It1& b, const It1& t, const It2& p)
          : bucket(b), table_end(t), curr(p) {}
        ⟨Hash_Table<T>::Iter operators 126c⟩
    };
```

The iterator and const_iterator aliases differ only in the use of const in their template parameters. The latter needs to declare its data members as an appropriate const_iterator type.

⟨Hash_Table *type aliases* 126b⟩≡
```
    typedef Iter<T,
        typename std::vector< std::list<T> >::iterator,
        typename std::list<T>::iterator
    > iterator;
    typedef Iter<const T,
        typename std::vector< std::list<T> >::const_iterator,
        typename std::list<T>::const_iterator
    > const_iterator;
```

The * and -> dereferencing operators need only the data member, curr, that iterates through the current bucket, returning a reference (or pointer) to the actual list element.

⟨Hash_Table<T>::Iter *operators* 126c⟩≡
```
    U& operator * () const { return *curr; }
    U* operator -> () const { return &(*curr); }
```

But the equality operators need to deal with both curr and bucket. Two iterators are equal if and only if the corresponding values of these two data members match.

⟨Hash_Table<T>::Iter *operators* 126c⟩+≡
```
    bool operator == (const Iter<U,It1,It2>& other) const
        { return bucket == other.bucket and curr == other.curr; }
    bool operator != (const Iter<U,It1,It2>& other) const
        { return bucket != other.bucket or curr != other.curr; }
```

The increment operators need to find the next element in the table, which may be in the same bucket or in a later one.

⟨Hash_Table<T>::Iter *operators* 126c⟩+≡
```
  Iter<U,It1,It2>& operator ++()        // prefix ++
 {
      ⟨make curr point to the next valid element 127b⟩
      return *this;
  }
  Iter<U,It1,It2> operator ++(int)      // postfix ++
  {
      Iter<U,It1,It2> result = *this;
      ⟨make curr point to the next valid element 127b⟩
      return result;
  }
```

To find the next valid element, we first move the `curr` iterator to the next element in the current bucket. If we've reached the end of that list, we search through the following buckets until we either reach the end of the table, or find a non-empty bucket.

⟨make curr *point to the next valid element* 127b⟩≡
```
  ++curr;
  while (bucket != table_end and curr == bucket->end()) {
      ++bucket;
      if (bucket != table_end) {
          curr = bucket->begin();
      }
  }
```

The initial iterator must refer to the first element in the first non-empty bucket in the table.

⟨Hash_Table *member function declarations* 122a⟩+≡
```
  iterator begin()
  {
      ⟨find non-empty bucket, and return iterator for its first element 128a⟩
  }
  const_iterator begin() const
  {
      ⟨find non-empty bucket, and return iterator for its first element 128a⟩
  }
```

We start looking in the first bucket. Once we've found a non-empty bucket, we construct an iterator that refers to its first element. If there are no non-empty buckets, we return our own `end()` iterator. As in `find`, `decltype` allows us to use the same code for both the plain `iterator` and `const_iterator` versions.

⟨*find non-empty bucket, and return iterator for its first element* 128a⟩≡
```
auto bucket = table.begin();
⟨ensure that bucket is not empty, if possible 128b⟩
if (bucket == table.end()) { return end(); }
decltype(begin()) result(bucket, table.end(),
                          bucket->begin());
return result;
```

We ensure a non-empty bucket by iterating `bucket` until we've either reached the end of the table or `bucket` is not empty.

⟨*ensure that* bucket *is not empty, if possible* 128b⟩≡
```
while (bucket != table.end() and bucket->empty()) {
    ++bucket;
}
```

Our `end()` iterators are just those whose `bucket` member refers to `table.end()` and whose `curr` member refers to the end of the list in the last bucket. In this case, the second constructor parameter is irrelevant.

⟨`Hash_Table` *member function declarations* 122a⟩+≡
```
iterator end()
{
    return iterator(table.end(), table.end(),
                    table.back().end());
}
const_iterator end() const
{
    return const_iterator(table.end(), table.end(),
                          table.back().end());
}
```

9.7 UNORDERED_SET **AND** UNORDERED_MAP **IMPLEMENTATION**

Just as our `Set` and `Map` implementations use a `Binary_Search_Tree`, `Unordered_Set` and `Unordered_Map` implementations use a `Hash_Tree`. Just as the `Set` declaration mirrors that of `Binary_Search_Tree`, the `Unordered_Set` declaration mirrors `Hash_Tree` with the same template parameters, and similarly, need not be explicitly shown.

But, like `Map`, the declaration of `Unordered_Map` is different enough to require some explanation. Like `Map` it has two template parameters, `K` and `V`, in place of `Unordered_Set`'s single `T`, and the hash function (`H`) and equality (`Equal`) parameters depend on the "key" type, `K`, rather than T. It also has a `pair`-like `element_type` and customized hash and equality functions that depend only on the keys (`hash_func` and `eq_func`, respectively. Not surprisingly, we can reuse `Map`'s `element_type` declaration here.

⟨*interface for* Unordered_Map 129a⟩≡

```
template <typename K, typename V, typename H = std::hash<K>,
                typename Equal = std::equal_to<K> >
class Unordered_Map {
private:
    ⟨Map's element_type definition 89⟩
    struct hash_func {
        H hash;
        int operator()(const element_type& x) const
            { return hash(x.first); }
    };
    struct eq_func {
        Equal eq;
        bool operator()(const element_type& a,
                        const element_type& b) const
            { return eq(a.first, b.first); }
    };
public:
    ⟨Unordered_Map aliases 132c⟩
    ⟨Unordered_Map functions 130a⟩
private:
    ⟨Unordered_Map data members 129c⟩
};
```

The only data member in either class is `table`, a hash table with the appropriate template parameters. `Unordered_Set` passes its template parameters along unchanged, but like `Map`, `Unordered_Map` needs to specify `element_type`, `hash_func` and `eq_func` as the `Hash_Table`'s T (element), H (hash function) and `Equal` (equality function) parameters, respectively.

⟨Unordered_Set *data members* 129b⟩≡

```
Hash_Table<T,H,Equal> table;
```

⟨Unordered_Map *data members* 129c⟩≡

```
Hash_Table<element_type, hash_func,eq_func> table;
```

9.7.1 Constructors/Destructors

The `initializer_list` and default constructors pass their arguments along to the corresponding `Hash_Table` constructors. The compiler-generated destructor and other constructors suffice.

⟨Unordered_Set *functions* 129d⟩≡

```
Unordered_Set(std:: initializer_list<T> init)
    : table(init) {}
Unordered_Set(int buckets = 1)
    : table(buckets) {}
```

⟨Unordered_Map *functions* 130a⟩≡
```
Unordered_Map(std:: initializer_list <element_type> init)
    : table(init) {}
Unordered_Map(int buckets = 1)
    : table(buckets) {}
```

9.7.2 Member Functions

Accessors

Similarly, the `size`, `empty`, `load_factor` and `max_load_factor` accessors let the corresponding `Hash_Table` functions do all the work.

⟨Unordered_Set *functions* 129d⟩+≡
```
int size() const { return table.size(); }
bool empty() const { return table.empty(); }
float load_factor() const { return table.load_factor(); }
float max_load_factor() const
    { return table.max_load_factor(); }
```

⟨Unordered_Map *functions* 130a⟩+≡
```
int size() const { return table.size(); }
bool empty() const { return table.empty(); }
float load_factor() const { return table.load_factor(); }
float max_load_factor() const
    { return table.max_load_factor(); }
```

As with `Set` and `Map`, the work of the `count` function is passed along to its counterpart, the only difference being that the `Unordered_Map` function passes a key-value pair (with a superfluous value—remember that searching in either the `Map` and `Unordered_Map` class uses only the key part of the key-value pair).

⟨Unordered_Set *functions* 129d⟩+≡
```
int count (const T& item) const {return table.count(item);}
```

⟨Unordered_Map *functions* 130a⟩+≡
```
int count (const K& key) const
    { return table.count(element_type(key, V())); }
```

The '[]' operator and `at` function are provided by `Unordered_Map`, but not `Unordered_Set`, and are implemented exactly as they are in `Map`. The '[]' operator inserts a dummy element with the specified key (the insertion is ignored if the key is already in the table, of course) and returns a reference to the corresponding value,

⟨Unordered_Map *functions* 130a⟩+≡
```
V& operator [] (const K& key)
{
    auto p = table.insert(element_type(key, V()));
    return p->second;
}
```

while the at function, which has both a const and non-const version,

⟨Unordered_Map *functions* 130a⟩+≡
```
V& at(const K& key)
{
    ⟨return value corresponding to key in this Unordered_Map 131b⟩
}
V at(const K& key) const
{
    ⟨return value corresponding to key in this Unordered_Map 131b⟩
}
```

merely searches for the specified key, returning the corresponding value (const version) or a reference to that value (non-const version) only if the key already exists in the table. If it doesn't, the function throws an out_of_range exception.

⟨*return value corresponding to* key *in this* Unordered_Map 131b⟩≡
```
auto p = table.find(element_type(key, V()));
if (p == table.end()) {
    throw std::out_of_range("nonexistent Unordered_Map key");
}
return p->second;
```

Mutators

The insert function (provided only by Unordered_Set), passes its work along to the corresponding Hash_Table function,

⟨Unordered_Set *functions* 129d⟩+≡
```
void insert(const T& item) { table.insert(item); }
```

as do the clear, rehash, and max_load_factor mutators in both classes.

⟨Unordered_Set *functions* 129d⟩+≡
```
void clear() { table.clear(); }
void rehash(int new_size) { table.rehash(new_size); }
void max_load_factor(float new_limit)
    { table.max_load_factor(new_limit); }
```

⟨Unordered_Map *functions* 130a⟩+≡
```
void clear() { table.clear(); }
void rehash(int new_size) { table.rehash(new_size); }
void max_load_factor(float new_limit)
    { table.max_load_factor(new_limit); }
```

This is also true for the erase function, but the Unordered_Map version must pass a dummy key-value pair in order to do the search.

⟨Unordered_Set *functions* 129d⟩+≡
```
void erase(const T& item) {table.erase(item); }
```

⟨Unordered_Map *functions* 130a⟩+≡
```
  void erase(const K& key)
     { table.erase(element_type(key, V())); }
```

9.7.3 Iterators

Both Unordered_Set and Unordered_Map use Hash_Table iterators as their own. As with Set (and for the same reasons), Unordered_Set uses only const_iterator.

⟨Unordered_Set *aliases* 132b⟩≡
```
  typedef typename
      Hash_Table<T,H,Equal>::const_iterator iterator;
  typedef typename
      Hash_Table<T,H,Equal>::const_iterator const_iterator;
```

⟨Unordered_Map *aliases* 132c⟩≡
```
  typedef typename
    Hash_Table<element_type,hash_func,eq_func>::iterator
      iterator;
  typedef typename
    Hash_Table<element_type,hash_func,eq_func>::const_iterator
      const_iterator;
```

⟨Unordered_Set *functions* 129d⟩+≡
```
  const_iterator begin() const { return table.begin(); }
  const_iterator end() const { return table.end(); }
```

⟨Unordered_Map *functions* 130a⟩+≡
```
        iterator begin()       { return table.begin(); }
  const_iterator begin() const { return table.begin(); }
        iterator end()         { return table.end(); }
  const_iterator end() const { return table.end(); }
```

PROGRAMMING EXERCISE

Reimplement the Hash_Table class using quadratic probing instead of chaining. The erase function will probably be the most difficult to write. Simply removing a value from the table will not work, as there may be another value with the same hash value placed elsewhere in the table because this bucket was already occupied. Replacing the value with a special "deleted" marker will work, but will not reduce the load factor, and you'll need to figure out how to keep the table from filling up with these markers.

CHAPTER 10

GRAPHS

In 1735, the citizens of Königsberg (now Kaliningrad) liked to amuse themselves on Sunday strolls by trying to cross each of the seven bridges in the city once and only once. Figure 10.1 is a sketch of the city

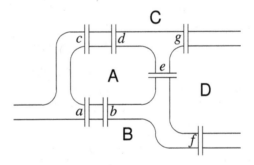

FIGURE 10.1 The seven bridges of Königsberg

as it existed at that time. They were never able to succeed, so they enlisted the help of mathematician Leonhard Euler, who not only proved that such a path was impossible, but also laid the foundations for the mathematical field of graph theory (the labels in the sketch are the same as in Euler's original paper).

A *graph* is a collection of *edges* and *vertices* (sometimes called *nodes*) joined by those edges. Figure 10.2 shows Figure 10.1 as a graph, with the land areas as vertices and the bridges as edges. A graph such as this, in which the edges represent two-way connections between the vertices, is called an *undirected graph*. A graph in which each edge is a one-way connection from one vertex to another is called a *directed graph*, or *digraph*. The edges in a graph may have numeric *weights*, which represent the distance

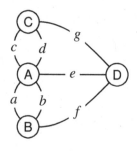

FIGURE 10.2 Figure 10.1 as a graph

between the vertices, or some other cost associated with going from one vertex to the other. Figure 10.3 is an example of a weighted digraph. In this

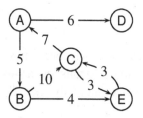

FIGURE 10.3 A weighted directed graph

graph, ABCE is a valid path, but ABCD is not. Also, the path BECA (with a combined weight of $4 + 3 + 7 = 14$) is "shorter" than the path BCA (with a combined weight of $10 + 7 = 17$), even though BECA passes through the extra vertex, E. A graph is said to be *connected* if, for any two vertices, there is a path between them. A directed graph is *weakly connected* if there is an undirected path between any pair of vertices, but *strongly connected* if there is a directed path between any such pair.

10.1 GRAPH REPRESENTATIONS

10.1.1 Adjacency Matrix

One way to represent a graph, whether directed or undirected is with an *adjacency matrix*. Figure 10.4 shows the adjacency matrix corresponding to the graph in Figure 10.3. The matrix indexes are the vertex names, and the entries in each row are the weights of edges from the row vertex to the column vertex. Empty entries indicate no edge from the row vertex to the column vertex. Unweighted graphs use boolean values or ones and zeroes (true/1 when an edge exists, false/0 otherwise). Undirected graphs have adjacency matrices that are symmetric around the up-left/down-right diag-

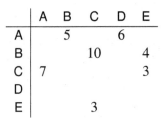

	A	B	C	D	E
A		5		6	
B			10		4
C	7				3
D					
E			3		

FIGURE 10.4 Adjacency matrix representation of the graph in Figure 10.3

onal. Since adjacency matrices are often sparse, a map or unordered_map is usually used to represent one.

10.1.2 Adjacency Lists

Another possible way to represent a graph is with *adjacency lists*. This representation consists of an array, indexed by vertex name, of linked lists containing the adjacency information for each vertex. Figure 10.5 shows

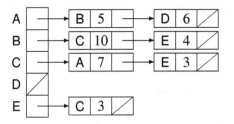

FIGURE 10.5 Adjacency list representation of the graph in Figure 10.3

the adjacency lists corresponding to the graph in Figure 10.3. Unweighted graphs need no field for the weight in the list nodes. Adjacency lists are particularly useful when it is necessary to iterate through all the neighbors of a vertex, or to save space when there is no practical way to store a sparse matrix.

10.2 TRAVERSALS

There are two traditional ways to traverse the vertices in a graph: *depth-first search* and *breadth-first search*. Both algorithms start their search from a single, given vertex, *v*, and assume a connected graph. If the graph is unconnected, the algorithms must be used separately for each of its separate parts.

10.2.1 Depth-First Search

A depth-first search follows a path as far as it goes from the starting vertex before exploring alternatives. The algorithm is tail-recursive.

Algorithm: *DFS(v)*

visit *v*
mark *v* as *visited*
for each vertex, *w*, adjacent to *v* **do**
    if *w* is not marked *visited* **then**
        DFS(w)

A depth-first search of the graph in Figure 10.3, starting at vertex A might visit its vertices in the order ABCED.

10.2.2 Breadth-First Search

A breadth-first search, on the other hand, visits all the neighbors of a vertex before exploring any other alternatives. The algorithm uses a queue to keep track of neighboring nodes not already visited.

Algorithm: *BFS(v)*

Require: *q*, an initially empty queue
visit *v*
mark *v* as *visited*
q.push(*v*)
while *q* is not empty **do**
    w ← *q*.front(); *q*.pop()
    for each vertex, *x*, adjacent to *w* **do**
        if *x* is not marked *visited* **then**
            visit *x*
            mark *x* as *visited*
            q.push(*x*)

A breadth-first search of the graph in Figure 10.3, starting at vertex A might visit its vertices in the order ABDCE.

10.3 EXAMPLE: TOPOLOGICAL SORTING

A *topological sort* is one that deals with a *partial ordering* in which a certain set of values have certain precedences, such as "both A and B precede D." This is useful where A, B, and D are all tasks that must be performed to complete a certain job. A topological sort orders these tasks in such a way that they can be performed sequentially but still meet the requirements imposed by the precedences. Figure 10.6 is an example of one such partial ordering. These tasks may be successfully performed in any of the sequences ACFBEGIHKDJ, ACDBEGHIKFJ, BACFDEHGIJK, BAEDCHG-FIKJ, as well as many others. But no sequence in which, say, G precedes E is allowable.

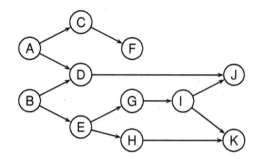

FIGURE 10.6 A partial ordering of tasks

The following algorithm uses a queue and a breadth-first search to perform the sort (an algorithm based on depth-first search is also possible). It first computes, for each vertex (task) the number of tasks it depends on. It then adds each task that has no predecessors to the queue (there must be at least one, or the job can never start). As the algorithm processes each task without predecessors, it decrements the predecessor count of each task that must follow it. Whenever that count becomes zero, it means that all possible preceding tasks have been processed, and the task is added to the queue. Once all the tasks have been processed, the algorithm is finished.

> **Require:** q, an initially empty queue
>   **for** each vertex, v, in the graph **do**
>   compute $pred[v]$, the number of predecessors of v
>   **for** each vertex, v, in the graph **do**
>   **if** $pred[v] = 0$ **then**
> q.push(v)
> $topnum \leftarrow 1$
>   **while** q is not empty **do**
> $v \leftarrow q$.front(); q.pop()
>   number v with $topnum$
> $topnum \leftarrow topnum + 1$
>   **for** each vertex, w, adjacent to v **do**
> $pred[w] \leftarrow pred[w] - 1$
>   **if** $pred[w] = 0$ **then**
> q.push(w)

Applying this algorithm to Figure 10.6 yields the sequence ABCDEFGHIJK.

10.4 EXAMPLE: SHORTEST PATH

A common problem with graphs is to find the path with the smallest total edge weights between a pair of vertices. There are a number of algorithms that solve this problem, the best known of which is *Dijkstra's algorithm*, developed by Edsger W. Dijkstra. Dijkstra's algorithm finds the shortest paths from a given vertex to all the other vertices in the graph. It divides the vertices into three categories: those that have already been completely dealt with (*visited*), those that have been looked at but not finished with (*fringe*), and those that have not yet been looked at (*unseen*). As a vertex is processed, its neighbors are added to the fringe (the *src* vertex is processed first), and the algorithm continues until all nodes reachable from *src* have been processed.

> **Input:** *src*, the vertex to start from
> **Ouput:** *distance*, the distances from *src* to the other vertices
> **Ouput:** *pred*, the vertices preceding each vertex in the shortest path from *src*
> **Require:** *unseen*, *visited*, and *fringe*, initially empty sets
> ⟨initialize *unseen* and *distance*⟩
> ⟨process *src* vertex and its neighbors⟩
> **while** *fringe* is not empty **do**
>   *v* ← the vertex in *fringe* with the minimum *distance*
>   ⟨process *v* and its neighbors⟩

Initially, all the vertices are unseen and are assumed to be an infinite distance away from *src*.

> ⟨initialize *unseen* and *distance*⟩≡
>   **for** each vertex, *v*, in the graph **do**
>   place *v* in *unseen*
>   *distance*[*v*] ← ∞

After marking *src* as visited and its distance to itself as zero, the algorithm moves each of *src*'s neighbors to the fringe, notes *src* as the neighbor's shortest path predecessor, and sets its distance from *src* as the weight of the edge joining them. These assignments are tentative, though, as it is possible that a shorter path through another vertex may be found later (for example, in Figure 10.3, the path BEC is shorter than BC even though B and C are neighbors).

> ⟨process *src* vertex and its neighbors⟩≡
>   transfer *src* from *unseen* to *visited*
>   *distance*[*src*] ← 0
>   **for** each vertex, *v*, adjacent to *src* **do**
>   transfer *v* from *unseen* to *fringe*
>   *pred*[*v*] ← *src*
>   *distance*[*v*] ← weight(*src* → *v*)

The fringe vertices are processed in a similar way. If a neighbor, *w*, is not yet in the fringe, it's treated exactly as the neighbors to *src* were, moving it to the fringe and setting tentative predecessor and distance values. If *w* is already in the fringe, however, its predecessor and distance values are updated only if the path through the current node, *v*, is shorter than the currently remembered distance.

⟨process *v* and its neighbors⟩≡
    transfer *v* from *fringe* to *visited*
    for each vertex, *w*, adjacent to *v* **do**
        if *w* is in *unseen* **then**
            transfer *w* to *fringe*
            pred[*w*] ← *v*
            distance[*w*] ← *distance*[*v*] + weight(*v* → *w*)
        else if *w* is in *fringe* **then**
            if *distance*[*w*] > *distance*[*v*] + weight(*v* → *w*) **then**
                pred[*w*] ← *v*
                distance[*w*] ← *distance*[*v*] + weight(*v* → *w*)

When the algorithm finishes, *pred* contains the shortest path from *src* to any other node, *v* (working backward from *pred*[*v*]), and *distance*[*v*] contains the distance of the shortest path from *src* to *v*.

You can better understand the algorithm by tracing its execution with an example. Let's use the graph in Figure 10.7, with vertex A as *src*. After

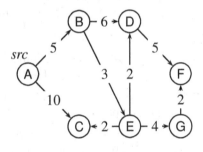

FIGURE 10.7 Shortest path example graph

processing A and its neighbors, B and C, the *distance* and *pred* tables have the following values:

	A	B	C	D	E	F	G
distance:	0	5	10	∞	∞	∞	∞
pred:		A	A				

At this point, only A has been visited, only B and C are in the fringe, and the remaining vertices are still unseen.

B is the closest fringe vertex to A, so it's the first one processed. Both of B's neighbors, D and E, are unseen, so they are moved to the fringe, and their entries in the *distance* table are set to 11 and 8, respectively, with their *pred* entries set to B.

The next vertex processed is E. Two of its neighbors, C and D are already in the fringe, but only D provides a shorter path, and its *distance/pred* entries are updated appropriately. G, being unseen, is added to the fringe.

The algorithm continues in this way, processing the vertices C, D, G, and F, in that order. C and F have no neighbors. Processing D moves F to the fringe, processing G finds that it is a better predecessor than D, and the algorithm ends with the following values in *distance* and *pred*:

	A	B	C	D	E	F	G
distance:	0	5	10	10	8	14	12
pred:		A	A	E	B	G	E

The shortest path from A to F, for example, is therefore ABEGF, with a distance/weight of 14.

10.5   A GRAPH **INTERFACE**

The STL does not provide a **graph** class, but in the interest of completeness, we provide one here with the following member functions:

Accessors

`vertices`	the set of all of the graph's vertices
`edges`	the set of all of the graph's edges
`neighbors`	the set of the neighbors of a given vertex an exception is thrown if no such vertex exists
`weight`	the weight of a given edge an exception is thrown if no such edge exists

Mutators

`insert`	insert a vertex or edge
`erase`	remove a vertex or edge

This class provides only **clear** out of the usual member functions; neither **size, empty,** nor iterators make sense here, although the **vertices, edges,** and **neighbors** functions each return an STL **set,** which can be iterated over. Also, the **vertices().size()** and **edges().size()** constructs can provide counts of the number of vertices and edges in the graph, respectively.

10.6   GRAPH **IMPLEMENTATION**

Our **Graph** class has three template parameters. The first, V, supplies a type for vertex names; the second, W, a type (usually numeric) for edge weights; and the third a value to be used as a default weight value for inserted edges (useful mostly for unweighted graphs). Edges are represented as pairs of vertices (first→second), so we define E to use as if it were a template parameter for an edge type.

⟨*interface for* Graph 141a⟩≡

```
template <typename V, typename W, W default_weight = W()>
class Graph {
private:
    typedef std::pair<V,V> E;          // edge type
public:
    ⟨Graph member functions 142a⟩
private:
    ⟨Graph data members and private functions 141b⟩
};
```

Some graph algorithms work best with an adjacency matrix, but others prefer adjacency lists, so we provide both, using an STL map for each (a sparse matrix for the former and an associative array for the latter). For efficiency, and to eliminate duplicate entries automatically, we use set instead of list for the lists. You may substitute the unordered types instead, if you prefer.

⟨Graph *data members and private functions* 141b⟩≡

```
std::map<V, std::set<V> > adj_list;
std::map<E, W> adj_matrix;
```

Many graph algorithms need to iterate through all of a graph's vertices or edges, so we maintain separate lists of these, using set instead of list for the same reasons as for adj_list. Much of the work in the mutators involves maintaining consistency among all the data members.

⟨Graph *data members and private functions* 141b⟩+≡

```
std::set<V> vertex_list;
std::set<E> edge_list;
```

10.6.1 Constructors/Destructors

No special constructors are needed. Nor is a destructor. The compiler-generated default constructor (creating a graph with no vertices or edges) is sufficient.

10.6.2 Member Functions

Accessors

To allow for iteration over a graph's vertices and edges, the vertices and edges functions return const references to vertex_list and edge_-

`list`, which have their own iterators. They can, indirectly, provide information about the size of the graph (i.e., the number of vertices and edges).

⟨Graph *member functions* 142a⟩≡
```
const std::set<V>& vertices() const { return vertex_list; }
const std::set<E>& edges() const { return edge_list; }
```

The `neighbors` and `weight` functions provide access into the `adj_-list` and `adj_matrix` data members, respectively. The former provides the list (`set`) of vertices adjacent to a given one; the latter provides the weight of the edge from the `src` vertex to the `dest` vertex. They both throw `out_of_range` exceptions (via `at`) if the specified vertex or edge does not exist.

⟨Graph *member functions* 142a⟩+≡
```
const std::set<V>& neighbors(const V& vertex) const
    { return adj_list.at(vertex); }
W weight(const V& src, const V& dest) const
    { return adj_matrix.at(make_pair(src, dest)); }
```

Mutators

To insert a vertex into a graph, all we need to do is add it to the vertex list and make sure that there is an entry in the adjacency list table corresponding to that vertex. Using the '`[]`' operator on the `adj_list` map has the side-effect of creating a new, empty entry in the table if one does not already exist.

⟨Graph *member functions* 142a⟩+≡
```
void insert(const V& vertex)
{
    vertex_list.insert(vertex);
    adj_list[vertex];
}
```

To insert an edge into a graph, both vertices must exist in the graph, so we insert them. The `dest` vertex must be added to `src`'s adjacency list, the edge itself must be added to the edge list, and the specified weight must be entered at the appropriate place in the adjacency matrix.

⟨Graph *member functions* 142a⟩+≡
```
void insert(const V& src, const V& dest,
                          const W& weight = default_weight)
{
    insert(src); insert(dest);
    adj_list[src].insert(dest);
    E edge(src, dest);
    edge_list.insert(edge);
    adj_matrix[edge] = weight;
}
```

To remove a vertex from a graph, we must remove it from the vertex list, and remove all traces of it from the adjacency list, adjacency matrix, and edge list.

⟨Graph *member functions* 142a⟩+≡
```
void erase(const V& vertex)
{
    vertex_list.erase(vertex);
    ⟨remove all traces of vertex from adj_list 143b⟩
    ⟨remove all traces of vertex from adj_matrix 143c⟩
    ⟨remove all traces of vertex from edge_list 144a⟩
}
```

Removing a vertex from the adjacency list table involves removing the entry corresponding to the vertex and removing any entries that refer to it in the other entries.

⟨*remove all traces of* vertex *from* adj_list 143b⟩≡
```
adj_list.erase(vertex);
for (auto p = adj_list.begin(); p != adj_list.end(); p++) {
    p->second.erase(vertex);
}
```

To remove all traces of a vertex from the adjacency matrix, we have to remove any element in the matrix for which the vertex is either the source (`first.first`) or the destination (`first.second`) of an edge (remember that a `map` iterator refers to a `pair`, the `first` element of which is the key—an edge in this case). We need the temporary, `tmp`, because the call to `erase` removes the current element, which invalidates the iterator. Using the postfix decrement operator when initializing `tmp` saves us a separate increment statement. It's a small saving, but this situation is exactly what the postfix operator was designed for.

The version of `map::erase` that accepts an iterator parameter is one not mentioned before, but it's useful here.

⟨*remove all traces of* vertex *from* adj_matrix 143c⟩≡
```
{
    auto p = adj_matrix.begin();
    while (p != adj_matrix.end()) {
        if (p->first.first == vertex
                or p->first.second == vertex) {
            auto tmp = p++;
            adj_matrix.erase(tmp);
        } else {
            p++;
        }
    }
}
```

Removing a vertex from the edge list is similar to removing an element from the adjacency matrix, temporary variable and all. Since the edge list is a **set** whose elements are pairs, the **first** part of each element is the edge source and the **second** part is the edge destination. If either of these are the same as **vertex**, the edge needs to be removed.

⟨*remove all traces of* **vertex** *from* **edge_list** 144a⟩≡

```
{
    auto p = edge_list.begin();
    while (p != edge_list.end()) {
        if (p->first == vertex or p->second == vertex) {
            auto tmp = p++;
            edge_list.erase(tmp);
        } else {
            p++;
        }
    }
}
```

To remove an edge, we need to remove the corresponding elements from the edge list, the adjacency matrix, and the adjacency list. It's necessary to make sure that the appropriate adjacency list entry exists before erasing **dest** from it so that a request to remove an edge starting from a non-existent vertex quietly does nothing rather than throwing an exception. We can't use the '**[]**' operator here instead of **at**, because it would create an unwanted new table entry when presented with a nonexistent **src** vertex.

⟨Graph *member functions* 142a⟩+≡

```
void erase(const V& src, const V& dest)
{
    E edge(src, dest);
    edge_list.erase(edge);
    adj_matrix.erase(edge);
    if (adj_list.count(src) != 0) {
        adj_list.at(src).erase(dest);
    }
}
```

Clearing a graph simply involves clearing all the data members, each of which has its own **clear** function.

⟨Graph *member functions* 142a⟩+≡

```
void clear()
{
    adj_list.clear();
    adj_matrix.clear();
    vertex_list.clear();
    edge_list.clear();
}
```

PROGRAMMING EXERCISE

Use the `Graph` class defined in this chapter to implement the algorithms described in the chapter.

A PROGRAMMER'S LIBRARY

As you progress in your career, you will accumulate your own library of computer science books. This appendix describes (roughly in order of importance) fundamental texts that every computing professional should have in his or her personal library. I have included only those books relevant to programming and data structures. A list of the seminal works on more advanced topics will have to wait for another day.

The Art of Computer Programming by Donald E. Knuth. The single most important reference for computing professionals. A proposed seven volume set, three of which (as well as parts of volume 4) have been published so far. These books contain the definitive explanation of every topic covered in this text,* and figure significantly in the bibliographies of every existing data structures book (particularly volumes 1 and 3). New copies are expensive, but well worth it in the long run.

Structured Programming by O.-J. Dahl, E. W. Dijkstra, and C. A. R. Hoare. Three prescient essays by three pioneers of computer science. Published in 1972, the first essay deals with structured programming techniques, the second with data abstraction, and the third with object-oriented programming. Interestingly, these were the primary programming paradigms of the 1970s, 1980s, and 1990s, in that order. The current state of the programming art may be blamed on the fact that this book has no fourth essay and no sequel. See also Dijkstra's *A Discipline of Programming*.

---

*Except graphs (Chapter 10), which will be covered in volume 4. Graph-related preliminary work for volume 4 can also be found in Knuth's *The Stanford GraphBase*.

The Psychology of Computer Programming by Gerald M. Weinberg. The first, and probably still the best study of computer programming as a human activity. The way programmers work has significantly changed since its publication, but most of Weinberg's observations and recommendations still hold true. There is a newer, "Silver Anniversary Edition" available, which I have not read. The new edition is priced significantly higher than the original.

The Mythical Man-Month by Frederick P. Brooks, Jr. This book covers much of the same ground as Weinberg's, but from a more anecdotal perspective. Brooks was the manager of IBM's OS/360 project in the 1960s, and brings this experience to bear in trying to come to grips with how best to handle programming teams and large software projects. The 20th Anniversary Edition also reprints his seminal "No Silver Bullet" essay, and includes new essays looking back at the impact of that essay as well as that of the original edition. The newer edition is not significantly more expensive than the original.

The Elements of Programming Style by Brian W. Kernighan and P. J. Plauger. Inspired by Strunk & White's *The Elements of Style*, this book demonstrates good programming practice by use of example programs taken from textbooks. Each program is critiqued, and then rewritten to illustrate a particular principle of programming style. The example programs are all written in either Fortran or PL/I, but should still be understandable by current computer science students. The principles, however, are universal. See also Henry Ledgard's *Programming Proverbs*.

Software Tools also by Kernighan and Plauger. A book that demonstrates good programming techniques by developing significant programs (the "tools" of the title), based on standard Unix utilities. The best available exposition of how to approach programs larger than those usually written for programming classes. You may prefer *Software Tools in Pascal* by the same authors.

How to Solve It by G. Polya. Not a computer science text, but the definitive work on problem solving in general. First published in 1945 and still in print. Need I say more?

Algorithms + Data Structures = Programs by Niklaus Wirth. An early text on data structures that explicitly sets out to embody the principles laid down in the first two essays in *Structured Programming* (listed above). The title says it all, and has never been improved upon. Later reworked as *Algorithms & Data Structures*. See also the author's *Systematic Programming*.

Programming Pearls by Jon Bentley. A collection of vignettes illustrating a variety of programming issues and techniques, but focusing on the application of "insight and creativity" to produce elegant rather than merely workable solutions. An excellent companion to *Elements of Programming Style* (listed above). The essays were originally published in *Communications of the ACM*. Also *More Programming Pearls*.

Be sure to keep your eye out for books that are not seminal, but are still interesting in their own right. Your tastes may differ, but my list includes *Electronic Life* by Michael Crichton; *Travels in Computerland* by Ben Ross Schneider, Jr.; *Computer by the Tail* by Donaldson, Stevens, & Becket; *A Fortran Coloring Book* by Roger Emanuel Kaufman; and *The Preparation of Programs for an Electronic Digital Computer* by Wilkes, Wheeler & Gill. This last is the very first programming textbook ever written, published in 1951. It has a surprisingly modern outlook, however, dedicating almost two thirds of its pages to the problem of reusable code (a lesson we still haven't adequately learned).

And don't forget fiction.

STL CLASS SUMMARY

T his appendix provides a summary of the STL container classes discussed in earlier chapters, and their member functions.

CLASS VECTOR<T>

Header: <vector>

Template Parameter: T—element type

Constructors & Assignment:

`vector(int sz = 0, const T& init = T())` $O(n)$
construct a `vector` with `sz` elements, each with the value `init`

`vector(const vector<T>& other)` $O(n)$
copy constructor

`vector(std::initializer_list<T>& init)` $O(n)$
initializer list constructor

`vector<T>& operator = (const vector<T>& other)` $O(n)$
assignment operator

Accessors:

`int size()` $O(1)$
the number of elements stored

`bool empty()` $O(1)$
`true` if and only if `size()` is zero

`int capacity()` $O(1)$
the number of elements for which storage is currently allocated; `capacity()` ≥ `size()`

`T& operator [] (int i)`	$O(1)$
the element at index i	
`T& at(int i)`	$O(1)$
the element at index i (bounds checked)	
`T& front()`	$O(1)$
the first element, `v.front()` $\equiv$ `v[0]`	
`T& back()`	$O(1)$
the last element, `v.back()` $\equiv$ `v[v.size() - 1]`	

Mutators:

`void push_back(const T& val)`	$O(1)$
append the value `val` as the last element	
`void pop_back()`	$O(1)$
remove the last element	
`void clear()`	$O(1)$
remove all the elements	
`void resize(int new_size, const T& init = T())`	$O(n)$
change the number of elements stored; set any new elements to `init`	

Iterators:

`iterator begin()`	$O(1)$
iteration starting point	
`iterator end()`	$O(1)$
iteration ending point	

CLASS LIST<T>

Header: `<list>`
Template Parameter: T—element type
Constructors & Assignment:

`list()`	$O(1)$
construct an empty `list`	
`list(const list<T>& other)`	$O(n)$
copy constructor	
`list(std::initializer_list<T>& init)`	$O(n)$
initializer list constructor	
`list<T>& operator = (const list<T>& other)`	$O(n)$
assignment operator	

Accessors:

`int size()`	$O(1)$
the number of elements stored	
`bool empty()`	$O(1)$
`true` if and only if `size()` is zero	

`T& front()`	$O(1)$
the first element	
`T& back()`	$O(1)$
the last element	

Mutators:

`void push_front(const T& val)`	$O(1)$
insert the value `val` as the first element	
`void push_back(const T& val)`	$O(1)$
append the value `val` as the last element	
`void pop_front()`	$O(1)$
remove the first element	
`void pop_back()`	$O(1)$
remove the last element	
`void clear()`	$O(n)$
remove all the elements	
`iterator insert(iterator pos, const T& val)`	$O(1)$
insert the value `val` immediately before `pos`; return the position of the new element	
`iterator erase(iterator pos)`	$O(1)$
remove the element at `pos`; return the position of the element that followed `pos`	

Iterators:

`iterator begin()`	$O(1)$
iteration starting point	
`iterator end()`	$O(1)$
iteration ending point	

CLASS STACK<T>

Header: `<stack>`

Template Parameter: T—element type

Constructors & Assignment:

`stack()`	$O(1)$
construct an empty `stack`	
`stack(const stack<T>& other)`	$O(n)$
copy constructor	
`stack<T>& operator = (const stack<T>& other)`	$O(n)$
assignment operator	

Accessors:

`int size()`	$O(1)$
the number of elements stored	
`bool empty()`	$O(1)$
`true` if and only if `size()` is zero	

T& top() $O(1)$
   the top element

Mutators:
  void push(const T& val) $O(1)$
    make val the top element
  void pop() $O(1)$
    remove the top element

Iterators:
  none

CLASS QUEUE<T>

Header: <queue>
Template Parameter: T—element type
Constructors & Assignment:
  queue() $O(1)$
    construct an empty queue
  queue(const queue<T>& other) $O(n)$
    copy constructor
  queue<T>& operator = (const queue<T>& other) $O(n)$
    assignment operator

Accessors:
  int size() $O(1)$
    the number of elements stored
  bool empty() $O(1)$
    true if and only if size() is zero
  T& front() $O(1)$
    the element at the front
  T& back() $O(1)$
    the element at the rear

Mutators:
  void push(const T& val) $O(1)$
    append val as the rear element
  void pop() $O(1)$
    remove the front element

Iterators:
  none

CLASS SET<T,COMPARE>

Header: <set>

Template Parameter: T—element type

Template Parameter: Compare—comparison function
(defaults to less<T>)

Constructors & Assignment:

set() $O(1)$
construct an empty set

set(const set<T,Compare>& other) $O(n)$
copy constructor

set(std::initializer_list<T>& init) $O(n)$
initializer list constructor

set<T>& operator = (const set<T,Compare>& other) $O(n)$
assignment operator

Accessors:

int size() $O(1)$
the number of elements stored

bool empty() $O(1)$
true if and only if size() is zero

int count(const T& val) $O(\log n)$
the number of elements matching val (either one
or zero)

Mutators:

void insert(const T& val) $O(\log n)$
insert the element val

void erase(const T& val) $O(\log n)$
remove the element val

void clear() $O(n)$
remove all the elements

Iterators:

iterator begin() $O(1)$
iteration starting point

iterator end() $O(1)$
iteration ending point

CLASS MAP<K,V,COMPARE>

Header: <map>
Template Parameter: K—key type
Template Parameter: V—value type
Template Parameter: Compare—comparison function
(defaults to less<K>)

Constructors & Assignment:

  map() $O(1)$
    construct an empty map

  map(const map<K,V,Compare>& other) $O(n)$
    copy constructor

  map(std::initializer_list
               <std::pair<K,V,Compare>>& init) $O(n)$
    initializer list constructor

  map<K,V>& operator = (const map<T>& other) $O(n)$
    assignment operator

Accessors:

  int size() $O(1)$
    the number of elements stored

  bool empty() $O(1)$
    true if and only if size() is zero

  int count(const K& key) $O(\log n)$
    the number of elements matching key (either one
    or zero)

  V& at(const K& key $O(\log n)$
    the element matching key; throws out_of_range
    exception if no element matches key

  V& operator [] (const K& key) $O(\log n)$
    the element matching key; inserts V() to match key
    if no element already matches key

Mutators:

  void erase(const K& key) $O(\log n)$
    remove the element matching key

  void clear() $O(n)$
    remove all the elements

Iterators:

  iterator begin() $O(1)$
    iteration starting point

  iterator end() $O(1)$
    iteration ending point

CLASS PRIORITY_QUEUE<T>

Header: <queue>
Template Parameter: T—element type
Template Parameter: Compare—comparison function
(defaults to less<T>)

Constructors & Assignment:

priority_queue() $O(1)$
  construct an empty priority_queue

priority_queue(const priority_queue<T>& other) $O(n)$
  copy constructor

priority_queue<T,Compare>&
  operator = (const priority_queue<T,Compare>&
                                                            other) $O(n)$

  assignment operator

Accessors:

int size() $O(1)$
  the number of elements stored

bool empty() $O(1)$
  true if and only if size() is zero

const T& top() $O(1)$
  the top element

Mutators:

void push(const T& val) $O(\log n)$
  insert the element val

void pop() $O(\log n)$
  remove the top element

Iterators:
  none

CLASS UNORDERED_SET<T,H,EQUAL>

Header: <unordered_set>
Template Parameter: T—element type
Template Parameter: H—hash function
(defaults to hash<T>)
Template Parameter: Equal—equality function
(defaults to equal_to<T>)

Constructors & Assignment:

unordered_set(int sz = 1) $O(1)$
  construct an empty unordered_set with sz buckets

```
unordered_set(const unordered_set<T,H,Equal>&
                                        other)         O(n)
  copy constructor
unordered_set(std::initializer_list<T>& init)          O(n)
  initializer list constructor
unordered_set<T>&
  operator = (const unordered_set<T,H,Equal>&
                                        other)         O(n)
  assignment operator
```

Accessors:

```
int size()                                             O(1)
  the number of elements stored
bool empty()                                           O(1)
  true if and only if size() is zero
int count(const T& val)                                O(1)
  the number of elements matching val (either one
  or zero)
float load_factor()                                    O(1)
  the current load factor
float max_load_factor()                                O(1)
  the maximum load factor allowed for the table
```

Mutators:

```
void insert(const T& val)                              O(1)
  insert the element val
void erase(const T& val)                               O(1)
  remove the element val
void clear()                                           O(n)
  remove all the elements
void max_load_factor(float new_limit)                  O(n)
  reset the table's maximum load factor
void rehash(int num_buckets)                           O(n)
  rehash the table to the specified number of buckets
```

Iterators:

```
iterator begin()                                       O(1)
  iteration starting point
iterator end()                                         O(1)
  iteration ending point
```

CLASS UNORDERED_MAP<K,V,H,EQUAL>

Header: <unordered_map>
Template Parameter: K—key type
Template Parameter: V—value type
Template Parameter: H—hash function
                        (defaults to hash<K>)
Template Parameter: Equal—equality function
                        (defaults to equal_to<K>)

Constructors & Assignment:

unordered_map(int sz = 1) $O(1)$
  construct an empty unordered_map with sz buckets

unordered_map(const unordered_map<K,V>& other) $O(n)$
  copy constructor

unordered_map(std::initializer_list
                    <std::pair<K,V>>& init) $O(n)$
  initializer list constructor

unordered_map<K,V,H,Equal>&
  operator = (const unordered_map<K,V,H,Equal>&
                                other) $O(n)$
  assignment operator

Accessors:

int size() $O(1)$
  the number of elements stored

bool empty() $O(1)$
  true if and only if size() is zero

int count(const K& key) $O(1)$
  the number of elements matching key (either one
  or zero)

V& at(const K& key $O(1)$
  the element matching key; throws out_of_range
  exception if no element matches key

V& operator [] (const K& key) $O(1)$
  the element matching key; inserts V() to match key
  if no element already matches key

float load_factor() $O(1)$
  the current load factor

float max_load_factor() $O(1)$
  the maximum load factor allowed for the table

Mutators:

void erase(const K& key) $O(1)$
  remove the element matching key

```
void clear()                                        O(n)
```
remove all the elements
```
void max_load_factor(float new_limit)               O(n)
```
reset the table's maximum load factor
```
void rehash(int num_buckets)                        O(n)
```
rehash the table to the specified number of buckets

Iterators:
```
iterator begin()                                    O(1)
```
iteration starting point
```
iterator end()                                      O(1)
```
iteration ending point

CHUNK INDEX

Underlined chunk numbers refer to where the named chunk is defined, the others to those chunks in which the named chunk is used.

INDEX